THE

GREAT

AMERICAN

DIVIDEND

MACHINE

HOW AN
OUTSIDER
BECAME THE
UNDISPUTED
CHAMP
OF WALL STREET

THE
GREAT
AMERICAN
DIVIDEND
MACHINE

HOW AN
OUTSIDER
BECAME THE
UNDISPUTED
CHAMP
OF WALL STREET

By Bill Spetrino

Humanix Books

www.humanixbooks.com
Boca Raton, FL, USA

The Great American Dividend Machine:
© 2015 Humanix Books

Interior: Ben Davis
Index: Yvette M. Chin

For information, contact:
Humanix Books
P.O. Box 20989
West Palm Beach, FL 33416
USA
www.humanixbooks.com
email: info@humanixbooks.com

Humanix Books is a division of Humanix Publishing LLC. Its trademark, consisting of the words "Humanix Books" is registered in the U.S. Patent and Trademark Office and in other countries.

Printed in the United States of America and the United Kingdom.

ISBN (Hardcover) 978-1-63006-034-3
ISBN (E-book) 978-1-63006-033-6

Library of Congress Control Number 2014958070

Contents

Acknowledgments

O F COURSE, NOTHING WOULD be possible without my loving and supportive parents, Patti and Bill Sr. Special thanks also to my sister, Denisa Grimm, my brother, Anthony, and my in-laws, Tony and Theresa Nero. As well, I give special thanks to my sisters-in-law, Marie Haffenden and Kim Spetrino, my brothers-in-law, Paul Haffenden and Jerry Grimm, my nephews, Brian and Billy Grimm and Ryan Haffenden, and to my favorite niece, Heather Haffenden.

Also, I offer thanks to all of my aunts and uncles: Bob and Jerri Spetrino, Art and Annelies Spetrino, and Annette Schroeder; and likewise to my cousins: Pamela Stockfish, Jeff Schroeder, Amy and Steve Schroeder, Greg and Melanie Spetrino, Jason Spetrino, Toni Montgomery, and Vicki Krueger.

Spending most of my life in the Mayfield Heights area has been an amazing experience. And it's been my privilege to have had the opportunity to be raised with incredible friends — those whom I've watched grow into well-respected adults and, most importantly, great parents.

Heartfelt thanks to all of my Lander Road Elementary School and Mayfield High School friends. I tip my cap to all of my coaches, especially Wally Mueller, Nick Lombardo, Jim Paradise, David Chordas, and Dave Todt. As well, I offer many warm thanks to some great teachers who've touched my life, most notably my third-grade teacher, Margaret Peterson, as well as Paul Gadke, Joe Santora, Jeffrey Smith, Ernie Safran, Carl Monastra, and the one and only Rod Meadows.

Another tip of the cap to all of my friends, teammates, and sports buddies who have given me great memories of laughter, sportsmanship, and friendship over the years, especially: Eileen Adams, Martha Allen, Carl and Tony Auletta, Susan Bascik, Willie Beers, Jack Berry, Joe and Liz Betschel, Miranda Borg, Jodi Braun, Jerry Burger, Joe Buzancic, Mike Caffery, Tony Carosella, Joe and Nancy Chapic, Frank Charlillo, Jack Ciccone, Lynette Clayton, Gale Crossley, Anthony DeCarlo, Douglas DeRoberts, Ben and Danielle DiMarco, Mickey Erickson, Kathy Estabrook, Domenic and Violet Ferritto, Domenic Ferrone, Joe and Renee Finucan, Chuck Gaglione, Joe Gallo, Bill Garcia, Nick Germano, Terry Gibbons, Lynn Gibson, Patti Goodnight, Becky Haffenden, Kelly Hanna, Susan Hill, Beth Hinkle, Mandy Hughes, Neal Intrater, Tammy and Jim Karmie, Nick and Deanna Kavaras, Karen Kelly, Bill Kump, Vince "the Mad Bomber" Lanese, Karl Langbhen, Diane Lipayne-Urda, Paul Loach, Mark and Cathy Lombardo, Ron Maholtz, Mike Maierson, Kimmie Malloy, Bernie Mandel, Pat Martucci, Tom and Eileen McTighe, Irene Molnar, Robert Montoni, Duckie Moore, Matthew Murphy, Mike Murphy, Bruce O'Hurley, Matt Palumbo, Michael Peskar, Joe Phillips, Stratt Pinagel, Larry Pinto, Darla Pirro, Dena Prater, Larry and Josie Puskas, Mike Ramacciatti, Jay Ranallo, Barrett Randell, Mike Rapposelli, Sherri Renne, Brian Roddy, Jeff Rudnick, Vince

Ruggieri, Monica Rus, Matthew Sachuk, Joseph Santoro, Linda Santucci, Mark Sassone, Dave Shaft, Dhaval Sheth, Randi Simmons, David Skarica, Mike Sloe, John Spetrino, Jen St.Clair, Jeff Stein, Mike Stoner, Tommy Tirabasso, Michelle Titsworth, D. Trevelyan Owens, Dan Valentino, Tim Valentino, Bett Verboten, Ilene Viny, Tom Wischmeyr, A. J. Wolnski, Rachel Woodruff, Sherry Woolard, and Nicholas Zanella.

All of those mentioned above have played a special role in shaping who I am today. For your love, kindness, patience, and camaraderie, I am most grateful.

At my 20-year high school reunion, I ran into a guy whom I hadn't seen since graduation. He said, "Bill, last I remember you were collecting baseball cards, selling tickets, and gambling. What are you doing now?" "The same thing," I replied.

Obviously, these three activities have played a huge role in my life. My thanks to all of those who've shared these worlds with me, sometimes in the most unconventional of ways, especially my sports-gambling and racetrack buddies: Jeffrey Kelman, Mike Razzante, Frank Marotta, and Tony Marotta. As well, much respect to those who trusted me in my first racetrack syndicate with Jeff Mahrer, especially: Pete DePaul, Mark Klang, Anthony Klang, Mike Thomas, Billy Sass, and Mike Trivisonno.

And to all of my loyal subscribers, who had enough faith in my investment savvy to unquestionably follow *The Dividend Machine* newsletter and *BIO* forum from their beginnings, I am forever grateful to all of you, notably: John Armstrong, Rob Brick, Chalker Brown, Tom Deaton, Amico DiFranco, David Dumais, Kelly and Heidi Erickson, Frank Ferritto, Jonathan and Candice Forte, Jay Coffsky, Greg Hanner, "Joe" Chang Jau Ho, Robert Hockensmith, Paul Jonson, Ann Iuen and Penny Kilby, Amit Kumar, Mike Mastrangelo, Angelo "Mister Le Marche," Gary McCartney, William

"Dave" and Kearstin Meadows, Roy Obreche, Dan O'Brien, Chris Rees, Art Riccio, David Rocchio, Wayne Schindler, Carl and Carol Scillia, Susan Sharp, Pat Sugrue, John "The Canuck," Mark Tretter, Leslie Wong, and Bob Wood.

I offer infinite thanks to Chris Ruddy of Newsmax and to my editors, Greg Brown, Mike Berg and Stephanie Gallagher, Aaron DeHoog, Jeff Yastine, Heath Ochroch, and Christian Hill, without whom neither *The Dividend Machine* newsletter nor this book would have been possible.

To the fine folks at Humanix Books, I extend many thanks to those who played a role in the writing and publishing of this book, most notably: Anthony Ziccardi, Andy Brown, Debra Englander, and Pamela Pantaleo for all of their assistance and guidance.

And last, but never least, I offer my greatest thanks to my supportive wife, Annette, and my amazing daughter, Stephanie. For all of your love throughout the writing of this book, and always, I am a lucky and blessed man to have you both in my life. I do it all for you.

INTRODUCTION

IF YOU SAT NEXT to me, an average-looking guy from Cleveland, Ohio, I would probably introduce myself by saying, "Hi, my name is Bill Spetrino and I grew up without a dime. But I figured out how to retire at 42, and now I'm a multi-millionaire living my life exactly the way I want to." It may not be politically correct, but it's a pretty good introduction, right? Well, guess what? You, too, could describe yourself the very same way. Okay, now that I've got your attention . . .

Even though you've picked up this book, you may be skeptical. Believe me, I understand your qualms. After all, there are thousands of investing books promising you financial security. Some of the authors are credible experts while others are written by people aimed at convincing you to put your hard-earned money into their funds or other investment accounts.

I'm in the business of making money, for myself and others. I make money with other people, not off of them. My subscribers pay me 26¢ a day — not the huge fees that they would be paying if they invested their money with a brokerage firm. In my monthly newsletter, *The Dividend Machine*, I tell people exactly how to invest their money. I identify and analyze the companies in which to invest — the very same companies in which I invest. And I do so using principles that are not flashy or sexy. I go against the grain and popular wisdom, and that is the key to my success. Knowing how to pick companies and stocks is my job. If you want a lifetime of paydays, earning it is your job. There's no interpretation or guesswork involved. I tell readers just like you exactly what to do to get spectacular returns.

Why should you trust me? My readers have put their trust in me for more than five years. I've been publishing *The Dividend Machine* since 2009, and I now have 80,000 subscribers and the newsletter has a below-market attrition rate. It's no accident — it's precisely because my information and investment counsel helps people gain the freedom to fulfill dreams they never thought possible.

You may be thinking: Why should I take your word for it? . . . Show me the results. Believe me, my readers are very happy with their profits. You can read some of their testimonials in the back of this book. And, my results are considered impressive. I have posted total returns of 191.6 percent over the past five years. My portfolio has had an average annual return of 21.8 percent and I've had 23 winning picks out of my last 23 conservative choices.

I pride myself on having a solid reputation. But, don't take my word for it. *The Hulbert Financial Digest* has been rating investment newsletters for more than 30 years. Over the last three years, my conservative portfolio was ranked #5 by Hulbert, due to its 21.8 percent annual return. In other words, $10,000 invested in this portfolio over the last three years would now be worth more than $18,000. Now, I know you're thinking that the stock market has been booming over this time period, so how does my portfolio perform in a bear market? Hulbert named *The Dividend*

Machine the #1 Low-Risk Newsletter in 2011, the last year the market was flat and down; the portfolio had a 19.8 percent return that year.

You can check out my documented track record at Dividend-Machine.com. And, just as I do with my newsletter, this book has a 90-day, money-back guarantee. I know that if you follow my principles, you will recoup the cost of this book and make so much more; you'll effortlessly become a successful investor. Again, that's why I'm offering you a money-back guarantee; I will refund the price of this book if you don't make money by following my strategies.

By reading this book, you are making an investment in your future. By educating yourself and taking control of your spending and your saving, you will be able to retire early, do whatever you want to every day, and not worry about the swings in the economy and stock market.

Now turn to chapter 1 and start learning how you can make money and secure your retirement.

PART I

Everything I Needed to Know I Learned from Watching Rocky (and Gambling)

The Three Words You Need to Understand

Before we get started on all the stuff you want to know about getting as rich as you can as fast as you can, let me throw three words in front of you: **Educate; Motivate; Entertain.**

Why are these my favorite, three little words? They sum up my role in life — particularly my role in *your* life right now. Those words represent what's going to happen as you read this book. If I can't keep you entertained, you'll put the book down. If I can't motivate you, you won't do what I know without a shadow of a doubt will benefit your financial life. Most of all, I have to educate you, because we all know the story about the benefit of teaching a person to fish rather than just handing over the fish. Frankly, that piece of advice is worthless. While you're busy teaching a guy to fish, he might starve to death. I KNOW that the only way to help another person out is to first serve up the fish and then follow it up with fishing lessons. So that's what I'm doing here. My decision to write this book is the equivalent of *me handing you the fish!* You're getting specific instructions on how to make money. By following my advice, you will make money. I'm also educating you about how to build up the right muscles and smarts (in my world, you've got to have brains and brawn) so that you can continue fishing on your own.

By now you probably realize that I'm an in-your-face kind of guy. I started gambling even before I went to schools so I'm going to talk a lot about baseball, horse racing, and other sports. My upbringing and background have defined my successes — and my failures — both personally and professionally. There's usually a lesson in my anecdotes; my stories may not be glamorous or exciting, but they're truthful. If my attitude occasionally rubs you the wrong way, that's okay. You don't have to like everything I say, but if you want to uncover the secrets to a secure financial future, you should listen to my advice.

We're All Like Rocky Balboa

To grasp how I was able to take an early retirement with total financial success and independence and gain a genuinely unique take on investing that works, indulge me for a moment and recall the movie *Rocky*. The protagonist was someone who came from nothing, and even though he had no one telling him he could make it, he trained ferociously and trusted his gut.

That's Rocky Balboa's story, but that's my story as well. Only my story is true — the real deal. In the movie, Rocky doesn't actually win — he loses to Apollo Creed in a split decision. However, Rocky went the distance despite getting knocked down, and that was as good as victory. That's how my life's been, and that's how real life is. We all can't be the World Heavyweight Champ, but if we continue to get up no matter how many times we fall (or are pushed down) — if we have determination and faith in ourselves — we'll come out winners. I know this because when I was a kid,

I had the opportunity to go to the fight between Muhammad Ali and the real-life inspiration for *Rocky*, Chuck Wepner. (In fact, there's a YouTube video of the fight and you can clearly see me sitting not too far from the ring.)

My buddy's dad, a professional gambler, promised his son and me that we'd get $1,000 each if Wepner knocked out Ali. Of course, Ali was the favorite, but in the 9th round the unexpected happened — Wepner managed to knock Ali off his feet. There it was — my first big score! What we couldn't see from our vantage point — what actually happened — was that Wepner stepped on Ali's foot, and followed with a shot to the ribs that threw him off balance, sending him backwards onto the canvas.

Wepner fought the good fight and lasted longer than anyone would've imagined, but in the end, Ali won in a TKO in the 15th round. Balboa and his real-life counterpart, Wepner, may not have been awarded the Belt, but they were champions in the eyes of their fans. And like them, I became the people's champ and defeated Wall Street by learning at an early age that I had to work, use the smarts I had, and trust my gut.

Let me spell this out another way. You're not getting a lesson about how to make money from some guy who grew up with a silver spoon in his mouth. I didn't have money handed to me when I was young. I didn't go to an Ivy League school, and I never had an "old boy" network to rely on. What I had was a dad who would kick my butt if I didn't follow his rules and a serious fear that I might wind up going nowhere. Forget having a trust fund — other than strong family values and my own instinct, I started out with barely anything to trust at all.

I don't care how corny you think this concept sounds, but we all have our inspiration. Rocky Balboa is mine. Maybe it's because I saw the real-life Rocky fight. Maybe it's because Balboa and I are both Italian guys whose chances for success seemed farfetched. Maybe I saw the movie at the time in my life when I really needed something to motivate me. Maybe after you finish reading this book, you'll come up with your own personal analogy. But right now, we're going to stick with Rocky.

The themes in the movie are the same principles that taught me exactly how to make money. These simple ideas are:

- Recognizing value that other people can't see (in Rocky's case it was in himself)

- Getting comfortable with sacrificing for as long as it takes until the wins start coming in

- Committing to a course of action and showing outstanding tenacity

That's it. Those are the basics. If you can grasp the concepts from one of the most famous underdog movies in history, you can follow the essentials of smart investing. I'm betting on you.

Recognizing Value Where Other People Don't

This is a very important concept for me as an investor and a point I hammer home in *The Dividend Machine* all the time. It's essential to remember this principle in life too! If you're just running with the crowd, doing what everyone else is doing, you're either going to be average, or worse — you'll wipe out.

Think about it for a second. If you're investing in whatever's hot at the time, how do you know that you're making a good bet? Is it a good idea to invest in a company just because it's popular? Who says it should be popular? Do you know why people adopt a herd mentality over a particular stock? Is there a reason or is a flock of sheep just moving in the same direction? If you don't know the answers to these questions, and your only measure of the value of your investment is that "everyone else is doing it," you're going nowhere. You may make some money for a while, but then the next popular stock will come along, the herd will follow it, and if you haven't dumped that stock at exactly the right moment, you've lost your money. You threw away your hard-earned money because you didn't know the real value of what you were backing. Even worse is when you're backing something trendy and get caught up in a phenomenon like the dot-com bubble. Under those conditions, you never stood a chance because you were backing something for which there was never any tangible indication of value — everything was speculative. There was absolutely no logic there!

Growing up, you probably heard the saying: Just because everyone else is doing it doesn't make it right. Or maybe you got the old: If everyone else jumped off the Brooklyn Bridge, would you do it too? If you follow the herd, the scenery never changes. You learned to second-guess yourself before you did whatever the herd was doing. You learned that acting like a jerk just because your buddies were doing it was stupid. There's no difference with regard to investing. In fact, the principles of good investing were hard-wired into your brain when you were a kid, but you just didn't know it. But, now I want you to recognize that one of the most important principles of successful investing is already part of your psyche. Don't go for what's popular simply because it's popular. Understand and know the true value of whom and what you're dealing with. You don't need an MBA from Harvard to understand the essentials; you can be just like me.

I didn't learn to recognize value because someone taught me. I did it out of necessity. I had to make my own money if I wanted it so I started young. My father helped me out with a few connections and I got a job as a ball boy for the Cleveland Cavaliers. I earned $1.25 per hour and got two tickets to each game that my dad skimmed off me in exchange for getting me the gig. Soon, I realized I wasn't going to make any real money that way. So I looked around myself and tried to see the value in my "situation," not just in the job I was given. The value of that arrangement was the proximity to the players and what went on behind the scenes. I figured out that there were three angles available to me and none of the other kids saw them, so I ran with those angles as fast as I could.

The first was that I could get unlimited autographs from the ball players. The other kids were afraid to ask the players for autographs, but I got them and then sold them to kids at school. Boom! Extra revenue. I also knew the players well enough to know what items they liked that I could get my hands on; I sold them boxes of candy that I bought, marking them up so I made a profit. The players appreciated the convenience of me getting them stuff and I made some money. Boom! More revenue. Finally, the basketball shoes were a goldmine. The players wore each pair of shoes only once and then they were "old," and no one cared about them. But I did; I took these gigantic, size fourteen, nearly pristine sneakers, which I got for free, and sold them to local college and high school players whose feet were just as huge as the NBA players. You guessed it . . . Boom! Big revenue. By seeing the value that no one else saw, what started as a $1.25 per hour job became a $30 per hour job.

I encourage you to look for value too, and I'll talk further about how to cultivate that in yourself. But even if you can't hone your ability to see value in what's around, you're covered because I'll be doing most of the work for you. Let's keep going.

Stick With It . . . And Don't Get Stuck!

Whether you say tenacity or guts, they're among my favorite words. You stick with something that you believe in, no matter what happens. Everyone can say you're crazy and you're making a big mistake, but if you know in your heart that you're right and you keep doing your thing, you've got tenacity. You don't give up before you've given yourself time to succeed. Now, that doesn't mean that if something truly isn't working you should stick with it on principle. If you're a rat on a sinking ship, you should realize that you're a sinking rat and that it's time to start running!

However, if something doesn't pay off at first but you know you've got accurate, long-range vision, that tenacity will let you grab your brass ring. You've got to be stubborn to get what you want. I'm stubborn as hell, which can annoy a lot of people, but I'm in good company. My tenacity is the same trait that Warren Buffett and all the other billionaires use every day.

My tenacity came in several forms that were all blended together by a major education in street smarts. Yes, I stuck with the job at the NBA, but it started earlier than that. It all started with gambling and baseball cards.

I already told you that I grew up poor, but I didn't tell you that being poor taught me two things: to look for the angle, and to be afraid. The first thing — looking for the angle — is not so different from finding value where others don't see it. Looking for the angle means *creating* value if you can. That's a very special talent. If recognizing value is like getting your college degree, finding the angle and creating value is like having a master's degree.

The second thing, being afraid, isn't so hard to understand. If you've got nothing, and then you've got something, you're going to be damned afraid of losing that something. When you're poor, there's no safety net. My old man taught me that. Being afraid taught me to be sure about everything I did and to never give people the opportunity to take anything from me that I wasn't willing to give them. Being afraid isn't being soft — it's being smart. If you grow up with money, which gives you a built-in safety net and a replacement for everything you lose, you're more likely to be soft. My advice is, if you think you fall into that category — even a little — find a way to find fear. Think about whatever could wipe out your security; live with this anxiety and keep it in the front of your mind. By doing so, you'll start to have an idea of the kind of drive that you need to find value and create your angles.

In addition to not having much when I was growing up, I also had a grandfather who gambled. I started gambling with him when I was four years old. I'm serious. We'd go to the track, but Grandpa would say that we were just going for a little walk. I made him take me by threatening to tell my grandmother that he was spending his days at the track. I kept bugging my grandfather until he showed me the racing sheets, explained how they worked, and gave me a few bucks so I could follow along and feel like I was doing what he was doing. Like grandpa like grandson, right? Wrong. What no one knew — even me — was that I had an unbelievable aptitude for math and logic.

As I got older and kept going to the track, I started to see patterns in how the horses and jockeys performed and how other people bet. I saw which horses would win and which ones wouldn't, no matter what the odds were. I knew a great horse that everyone was betting on to do well would do poorly if the jockey wasn't any good. I bet against the grain and started winning. It took me a while to trust what I saw in front of me (all those patterns and the truth behind my anti-logic), but I stuck with it and it paid off.

My father wasn't happy about the gambling and tried to discourage me. He handed me $500 and said, "Ok, son. You think you're a gambler? Let's see how you do." He wanted me to fear gambling because of the potential to lose all my money and *never* see that cash again. Dad's lesson, though well-intentioned, was actually a big mistake; it backfired. He expected me to blow the $500 that he gave me, but instead, I turned it into $5,000! My old man was right about gambling, though — it can ruin you. But I'm lucky enough to have a particular kind of brain that is a unique blend of fear, aversion to risk, mathematical acumen, and creativity. For this reason, following my lead when it comes to investing gives you a safety net you probably never had.

When I was just a little older — probably about seven years old — I got involved with baseball cards. My dad, who could hustle with the best of them (but never advocated taking advantage of people, particularly those who couldn't afford it), couldn't believe what I was doing. I had a bunch of baseball cards like all the other kids. I learned pretty quickly, though, that when another kid would see my collection and try to trade cards with me, he was trying to get some of the good ones I didn't even know I had. I thought to myself: No way! I paid for these cards so I'm not swapping them for nothing. I didn't give a damn about those cards, but when I realized that the other kids did . . . Well, that was an entirely different story. Following my dad's lead, if a kid from an affluent family wanted a specific card, he had to pay for it. Those cards had a high enough perceived value so the kids were willing to pay up. I sold a Sam McDowell card for 35¢ and bought seven more packs of cards. My father couldn't believe it when he saw the pile of cash (and the six shoeboxes of cards) I had earned from assessing perceived value versus actual value. (I had earned around $36.) At that tender age, somehow it all made perfect sense to me.

Okay, so those are a few examples of how I tapped into my innate resourcefulness and common sense in order to find the angle. But then I learned to *create* the angle. When that happened, my dad knew that gambling wouldn't ruin me.

Gambling is like being in the jungle — only the strongest survive. But I was thriving, not merely surviving. Most people think that gambling is all about knowing the numbers and mastering the statistics. While those skills are important, I learned that gambling requires a certain perspective. You have to understand all the variables at play. If you want to gamble successfully (and now, you should assume that I'm referring to "investing" when I say gambling) you have to make knowing the variables your business. You have to make it your life's calling. And once you know what the variables are and you've gotten the information you need from them, you have to know how to use them. I hung out with a few pro gamblers and picked up the principles, but then I did it my way. It was work, but it paid off and gave me the edge I needed.

In 1976, I started betting on college football; I began thinking about what factors would change a game's outcome. I wanted an edge and I quickly realized that weather could have a big impact. I knew that one of the major variables when betting on a football game was the condition of the turf. There was no weather channel in 1976. And back then I didn't have a smartphone to look up all the data that people now post online about things like the weather or the health of the guy who mowed the field. I didn't want to spend even a penny before I made anything on the game, and making long-distance calls to the 45 cities where games were being played would have cost me an extra $35 to $40 each week. But, directory assistance was free then, so I would call the local "information" in the town or city where the game was taking place. Back then you'd just dial the area code, then 555-1212. I'd tell the operator that I needed the number to the Holiday Inn, and I'd say I was thinking of coming in that weekend for the game, then I'd ask about the weather. To the operator, it was idle chit-chat. But to me, that was vital information that I needed to have the edge, and it was free. I would then know if a team that didn't play well on a muddy field was going to have a good or bad game.

In 1976, Princeton was playing Columbia in New York. This time the operator told me that it had been raining incredibly hard and said the game might be cancelled. Now, football games are almost never cancelled because of weather, so I knew that it must have been raining really hard and the field was in bad shape. Princeton was the favorite, and the combined total points for the game was supposed to be 36. Taking the "over/under," I bet $300 that the combined total would be under 36 because the field would be a mess and both teams would have trouble scoring. I was right. The combined score was 15, which was well under the 36-point total. So I won $300 — my biggest score ever. The extra information (in this case, the weather) helped me to win. I knew the statistics, I had the math, and I made sure I got the scoop on the variables through ingenuity. I *had* to know all that stuff because I was always afraid. I absolutely couldn't afford to lose, which meant I was really fearful of losing. These two factors gave me the boost I needed to make solid decisions that would yield good returns. That's how I learned to gamble as a kid, and how I later learned the essentials of investing without the benefit of an MBA.

You Can't Get Something if You Won't Give Anything Up

The concept of sacrifice is a funny idea for some people. They think it's a noble, saintly, even character-building thing to do. Even so, most people won't do it. Giving up something that has any value (perceived or otherwise) is a concept that's practically unheard of in the US. However, if you want to come out a winner, you're going to have to sacrifice something. You just do it. You make the sacrifice, you feel the pain, and then you see the results. With regard to investing, the results are more paydays. Sacrifice requires as much faith in investing as it does in any religious setting. But, what exactly do I mean by that?

If you sacrifice your spare time, which is the most important commodity of all, you can have a side business to earn extra cash. If you sacrifice your need for status, you can drive a cheaper car. If you sacrifice a few creature comforts every month, which could be your expensive coffee drinks or your cigarettes, you're going to save money. All that money, which doesn't seem like much when you're spending it, adds up. And that little bit of money, once it's invested, grows. And if you keep feeding that growing machine, you're going to see that by making sacrifices now, you'll be in a very secure position in the future. I'm using these examples of very small sacrifices so I can make it clear that absolutely anyone can start using my principles immediately. You don't need a big nest egg to start investing. You don't need to be a big shot to become a bigger shot. You can be in the same position I was when I started building my dividend machine.

It all started when I first got married and was selling insurance. I wasn't making much money and we weren't living the way I wanted to. I wanted the American dream, thinking it was something outside of myself. Then I realized that I had to figure out precisely what I wanted and where I was headed. My wife and I talked about this idea and I realized I had a clear vision of exactly what I wanted. I wanted to live the way I chose, no strings attached, not answering to anyone, and having total financial independence by the time I was 35 years old. But it would take sacrifice on both our parts, because every extra bit of money we could save would have to go into the investment project I was formulating. And we would never touch the capital — only the dividends from the investments. My wife agreed and we were up and running. I knew that I was going to retire at age 35 and be a free man, with total control over my own time, money, and life. I wanted to be the master of my own destiny.

Only my plan didn't work.

Rocky didn't win his first time in the ring. My investments were profitable, but I was self-employed and needed money to live; I couldn't reinvest. I believed in myself, though, and I had staying power, so I got back up off the mat. The bell hadn't rung yet! I kept going and my decision to keep moving forward paid off. Seven years after the goal I originally set for myself, my dividend machine was chugging along perfectly, as planned. I was in control of my money; it wasn't controlling me. I was independently wealthy and had created the safety net I had never had, both for myself and my family. And, sorry, but as Frank Sinatra would say: I did it my way.

I now have the two most valuable assets in the world: time and money. I have a life that is balanced spiritually, emotionally, mentally, and physically. I never sacrificed the long-term for the short-term. The money isn't the end goal. The money provides the opportunity to have a life where all the important elements are in harmony. I know that staying in balance is about developing a good blend of hard work and fun. I've proven to myself that when I am knocked down, which happens to absolutely everyone, I have what it takes to get back up. I keep focused and push on through trial and error until I succeed. I wanted the freedom of calling the shots and taking control of my life and not having to rely on a boss, and I achieved it.

Okay Bill, Now What Do We Do?

Now we're going to get into the nitty-gritty of how I approach money, investing, and feeding my dividend machine. I've got to be honest with you: You're never going to be me. And I'm never going to have whatever talents you have. But, if you're interested in having the abundance of time and money and life-balance that I've achieved, I'm here to help you get it. Go ahead and question everything I say, but give me a chance. I'm not here to sell books. That's not how I make my money. I believe that we all have a purpose in life. Mine was to find my own formula that allowed me to earn everything I now have, to be able to provide for my family, and to teach my daughter how to take care of herself. I also wanted to give other people a fighting chance to live the same American dream that I do. You should want to give back to your community. If you bought this book, you're part of my community. When I was starting out, other people gave me guidance and helped me to hone my natural talents. It takes a village to make a millionaire; at least it did for this one. I'm giving back by educating, motivating, and entertaining.

Now it's time to begin with the basics. I want you to start thinking about the value of money. It's easy to say that you want more of it, but why? What's so good about being rich?

Keeping My Word Led Me to a New Career

During the summers when I was a teacher, I was selling term insurance. I had met someone and told him to call me if I could ever help him. This guy called me from overseas and said he needed four tickets to the Neil Diamond concert, Now, I wasn't in the ticket business — that was the last thing I intended to do given that my father was in that business. But I had given him my word, so I made some phone calls and found the tickets. I ended up making $200 and began thinking . . . There were probably 4,000 people selling insurance in Ohio, but only half dozen people selling tickets. I got into the ticket business pretty quickly. Since I knew baseball very well, I knew which games were in high demand. I started talking to the ticket brokers and negotiating my deals. It was a great time because the Cleveland Indians made the World Series that year. I earned six figures just from selling tickets. It was the only year I ever made six figures before I became a millionaire from my investing.

2

Money Is Freedom

MONEY AND POWER ARE the ultimate drugs. Forget all the substances that fall into the category of "highly addictive and unbelievably bad for you." Money and power head the list. But are they intrinsically bad for you like a particular drug, or are they addictive but useful? Or even more to the point: Are they *good* for you? The answer is that you determine how money and power impact your life.

I realize that this comment might seem a little glib or remind you of a new age aphorism. It may sound that way if you haven't ever asked yourself these kinds of questions: What's the true value of money? What do you dream about when you're working toward financial success? Do you want fast cars and fancy watches? Are you looking for mansions in Miami or private jets and ski trips in Aspen? Or does money mean something else to you?

If you're focused on material wealth — acquiring stuff for the sake of acquiring it — I hate to burst your bubble, but if that's what you think money's all about, you've got it all wrong. Here's the absolute truth that I have realized, having been both impoverished and well-off: At the end of the day, being wealthy is not about being able to flash around evidence of what you can buy. It's about having power. But, despite what others may think, it's not about having the power to control other people or bend situations to your liking.

Having money is about having the power to achieve and maintain your freedom. This means that you have the freedom to choose to live as you want, in a way that lets you be *who* you want to be, and not just own what you decide to buy.

The Value of the Dollar

Okay, let's examine this thesis a little more. Let's talk about being rich. People always say they want to be rich, or if they're rich, they want to get richer. Why? What's the value of being rich? Is the value of being rich any different from the value of money? With so much social pressure, pop-culture, and emotion wrapped up in the idea of being rich, the concept has actually lost a lot of its real meaning. I would bet right now that if I asked you why you want to be rich, you wouldn't have an answer beyond the fact that it would make your life easier. In some ways it will. In other ways it won't. Before you decide to embark on changing your financial future, you should ask yourself exactly what you want to do with the money you earn.

When I resolved to change my life and make the necessary sacrifices and lifestyle choices to do so, I knew why I wanted to do it. I knew that I had a clear goal: retire by the time I was 35 years old (a goal that was achieved seven years late, but still achieved). I wanted to retire young so I could enjoy what I considered to be the fundamental parts of my life (my family, my wife, my kid, my friends, playing sports) without having to relegate them to nights and weekends. I didn't want a fancy life, but I wanted one that would allow me to stop and smell the roses. By the time I was 42, I had it, thanks to dividends. Of course I kept going, using my own investment principles to add to my wealth, but it was always to feed that core need that I just described. I've never done anything related to investing or wealth management so that I could have fancy cars, a flashy house, or the latest gadgets. I'm just not that kind of guy.

I'm not criticizing you if you're into more material things than I am. If you say that you want wealth because you want to have every Apple gadget and a fleet of luxury cars, that's fine. That's your thing. But accept that tendency in yourself when you start investing. Knowing why you're changing your life and the way you look at your relationship to money is going to be a huge part of your success.

Remember how I talked about tenacity? It's damned hard to be tenacious when you're waiting for the first dividends to come in if you don't have a *very specific* goal in mind. If your goal isn't personalized, it won't be enough to hang your dream on. You'll run the risk of asking yourself: How did I get here? (Apologies to the Talking Heads.) You'll run the risk of bailing out before you've gotten to your goal. It's human nature. So set a goal that accurately reflects who you are. WHO you are is the basis of WHY you want to invest. Being honest with yourself will bring you the success you seek.

Money Is a Tool That Builds the Dream — Not the Dream Itself

Okay, now that I've said that whatever you choose as your goal and your reason for wanting to have more money is fine, I'm going to add a caveat: Money is a great servant and a lousy master. If you're interested in earning money for money's sake — in other words, if the money itself is the ultimate goal — you'll never have enough. You'll never be happy because you will be letting the accumulation of wealth rule your passion and your self-worth.

If, on the other hand, you want money to be your servant, you need to have it to serve your needs. Those needs are the goals you set. Setting a goal of owning a fleet of luxury cars is a better goal than just wanting to be rich, because you've set up an identifiable and tangible finish line for yourself. Once you've reached that finish line, then you can set a new one. But wanting to "be rich" is meaningless. Even worse, it's an opportunity for heartache and just plain making yourself crazy. "Being rich" is an ephemeral goal. Stick to the tangibles or specific lifestyle choices and you'll be in much better shape.

For me, freedom is *not* just another word for nothing left to lose (yeah, it's another music reference); freedom is *everything*. It's the basis of every single choice I make and the foundation of what I guess I'd refer to as my lifestyle. I use the concept of freedom as one of my core criteria for decision-making. If I really want something, or want to do something, but getting there will make me compromise my ability to behave, dress, speak, or interact with others in the way I want to, then I DON'T DO IT. Freedom is my dream. Freedom is also my reality, and having wealth is the tool that I used to build that dream and make it my everyday life.

Have you ever thought about what freedom means to you? If you didn't have work obligations and no one was dictating your every move, what would your life look like? I bet that many of you can't even imagine this situation because it seems like such a pipe dream. Maybe you joke that if you won the lottery, you would quit your job and move to Tahiti. No, you wouldn't. Think again. If you had total freedom to do whatever you wanted to, what would you do? You need to have an answer before you continue reading this book. Your response may change as you accumulate greater wealth, but you need a starting point.

Why do you need to answer this question? You're going to have some money soon, and you must know why you want it and what you're doing to do with it. If you can't answer the question, you're going to get stuck. You'll get confused. You'll make bad decisions and you may have to start all over again. That's not the worst thing in the world, but don't you want to use your time wisely? I know I do. I know it because that's what my freedom is all about: having the time to do what I want with the people I value. My time is my freedom and my freedom is my time. Chew on that concept. In fact, I'm going to give you a few minutes to consider everything I just said.

Okay, have you finished mulling the question over? Do you have at least some idea about why you're on a journey to acquiring wealth? I hope so. I'm going to assume you do. Before we move on, I'm going to repeat myself. I know it's annoying to hear the same thing over and over, but essential to creating your own dividend machine is understanding these words: Money is a great servant and a lousy master. This is crucial. You can never forget that the goal is for you to be in charge of your life and your future, and money is just a means to an end. It's a tool, a mechanism, a machine . . .

You rule the money, not the other way around.

Doesn't sound like groundbreaking advice to you? Take a minute and think about how many people you know (including yourself) who really talk the talk and walk the walk I'm putting out there. You probably know people who work like maniacs to get as much money as they can. They might even be great at what they do and make a pretty substantial salary. But what good is a big fat salary if you're tied down to a job and a certain lifestyle that controls you instead of the other way around? Have you ever heard the phrase "golden handcuffs"? It means that what you've got may be really shiny and pretty from the outside, and may even be worth a lot of money, but you're a prisoner of something to get it. If you're keeping up with me and the philosophy I'm talking about here, you probably stopped when you read the word "prisoner." What good is a big house or a fancy car today if you don't know exactly when or how you're going to retire in some version of tomorrow?

Money isn't the goal — it's the way to reach a goal. Money is the way to build a secure foundation to live life the way you want. Understanding this concept is crucial to achieving financial and personal independence.

The Great Value in Being Conservative

To get the most of out of your dividend machine, you must grasp that making money and having money are two completely different concepts. If you want financial independence, or maybe just to overcome a circumstance in which you find yourself, you must embrace this concept. Being rich and secure isn't about what you buy. It's about what you can buy, what you can do, how you will take care of yourself and your loved ones . . . all because you've held on to your resources. I'll say it again: Making money and having money are two completely different concepts. Let me explain this further.

I'm going to start by saying something that may sound discouraging, but give me a minute to make my point. Not everyone can make a lot of money solely from their paychecks. Making a salary in excess of six figures is pretty damn difficult if you're not in sales, you don't own your own business, you're not a doctor, a dentist, an attorney, or aren't in some other high-paying field. You can work incredibly hard and still never come close to seeing the numbers you want on those paystubs. There are many terrific professions that pay very respectable salaries, but not the mega-earnings of some of the careers I've mentioned. Clearly, being married in a two-earner family is a huge advantage since you have two salaries coming in every month. (In this case "you" is plural — don't forget that. And two people can have two very separate sets of goals!)

Still, the reality is that there's a cap on how much money many of you can make. It all rests on your individual talents and your willingness to sell something, either for yourself or somebody else. Luckily, *having* money requires a different skill set.

I'm living proof that having money isn't about what you make, so much as it's about what you save. And I learned that once you've saved, your goal is to NEVER SPEND THE PRINCIPAL. After you've built your dividend machine and have done a good deal of reinvesting, then perhaps you could tap into your dividends. Until then, remember: Having money comes from investing, and from investing comes security and freedom. **You'll never spend your way to security**.

Small Futures for Big Spenders

My annual family income was only $100,000 one year before I became a millionaire. But we lived wisely and below our means for about 17 years in order to build up our savings. And we still do! We did it because I had a laser-like focus on saving money and building a dividend machine. You need to save a minimum of 10 percent of what you make, regardless of your income. Every time you get money, put aside 10 percent. That's probably the most essential part of my strategy. (In fact, all of you parents should be encouraging your children to do this when they're still living at home and not paying rent.)

Invariably, everyone can be classified as either a spender or a saver. If you're a saver, chances are you don't earn large sums of cash. Conversely, those who earn a lot feel they should spend a lot. Some earners make their money last a long time because their incomes are so big they can't overspend, no matter how hard they seem to try. But if you're more interested in *having* money than *making* money, you have to learn to save more than a spender ever will. Obviously, a person who makes a lot of money and is a saver will do best. But if you're smack-dab solid in the saver subset, breaking out of your earning rut and changing your financial destiny is about how fast you can compound your money at the lowest risk possible.

There's a reason "the rich get richer and the poor get poorer," and the explanation is pretty simple. The analogy I like to use is that people who exercise and eat right get healthier, and those who don't get unhealthier by the second. The answer is so straightforward that people don't believe it is real. To succeed, you have to have good habits. Good eating and sound exercise habits are the same as good financial habits. If you stuff yourself full of junk food, you'll never get in shape. If you spend all your money as fast as you get it, you'll never get rich. That simple analogy suddenly makes sense, right? Stick to a pattern that you know will pay off and no matter how long it takes to get there, you'll eventually get there. You may want to lose weight in two months. So what if it takes six? If you modify your diet and stick with an exercise program, you will make it! The same principle applies to your relationship to your wealth. If you're trying to increase your wealth, you have to follow some good habits and stick with them. You may not make it in the time frame you originally set (I didn't), but you *will* get there.

The key to understanding how the rich get and stay rich is accepting that you don't have to be flashy to enjoy your money. Personally, I detest the pseudo-rich — the wannabes, who can't seem to enjoy their money without shoving it in everybody's face. These people are always buying the so-called "best" of everything, just to show they can. They present the image that says: I'm rich, I don't need to bargain shop. Well, see how that works out 10 years from now when you're ready to retire and you're sitting there thinking: Where the hell did all my money go? A lot of these spenders don't realize how much their lifestyle is really costing them and preventing them from accumulating more wealth for later.

For example, I understand why people really like to live in California or New York. But the people living in those states have to understand how much they're paying in taxes and how expensive it is to buy a home in these regions. They may have a six-figure salary, but after paying 40 percent of it to cover taxes and the cost of living, they might only have $70,000 left. They want the flashy house in the fancy area to show off, but they really can't afford it.

On the other hand, I don't have a problem with the truly rich. You see, it's not about having money or not. It's the attitude that people have toward money that makes me judge them. I draw the line based on that skill of having money. The truly rich understand it's not important to show off your wealth by spending big. It's important to keep that wealth, and the freedom it gives you, by saving whenever you can. When I see my mechanic or landscaper, they have NO idea I have any money. I constantly try to get the best price, and if I talk about my business, I talk about it struggling. I never broadcast my wealth. I'm always looking for a deal and finding small ways to save big in the long run. For example, not drinking soda has saved me BIG money. And I never turn my nose up at a bargain. I almost always use a coupon or get a discount when I'm dining out. Saving money is satisfying for me because I understand how those dollars add up when it's time to invest. That is not to say that I will *ever* cheat someone out of his or her fair value or price. I'll never take advantage of anyone. I'm interested in what's fair and how I can make it work for me.

I once had a friend with whom I was considering going into business. It seemed like we were on the same page until he said one thing that made me take a giant step back. He told me, "I'd rather make $40,000 and have people think I make $80,000, than the other way around." That told me my friend was a spender. Looking a certain way to the outside was the whole point for him. He thought it was more important to look rich than to be rich and to spend that money rather than having that money.

As my other friend Mac would say: This guy's lifestyle was a case of "big hat, no cattle." Like me, Mac always lived below his means and never let anyone know how much he earned. Except for two other friends and myself, nobody knew he had a lot of money. He refused to drive a Corvette or do any other flashy things the pseudo-rich will do to show off their bank accounts.

For Mac, just like for me, it's always been about saving and living comfortably, but below our means. Most people fail in personal finance because they are spenders. Now, I'm not saying you have to be a monk and live on bare-bones rations — there's no freedom in that. But you have to remember that real wealth comes from having and saving. Before you buy something, ask yourself: Is the spend really worth it? You have to investigate why buying what you buy is important to you. *Money you're spending is money you're not investing.*

The Magic Ingredient . . . Ain't Magic

Okay, back to brass tacks. If you're reading this book, you're looking for advice about how to make an effective plan for yourself to increase your wealth and achieve freedom in your life. That means you're already on the right track.

We've already explained that the first thing you have to do is to figure out not just what you want, but why you want it. We've already gone through how and why money is just a tool that helps you achieve power and freedom in your life. Now we need to talk about the focus, discipline, and drive you need to save, invest, and accumulate wealth in a smart way. My focus and drive was passed to me by my father thanks to a conversation that came out of the blue.

It happened when I was at the first real job I had. I was hired by Citicorp (now Citigroup) as an auditor making $19,000 per year. That may not sound like much, but to a 23-year-old kid that was big bucks, especially back then!

I was excited because I had a secretary, a nice office, and a job that made me feel important. Truth be told, I felt like a bit of a hot shot. I remember calling my dad after my first day of work. As I bragged about my office with the window and my big salary, my dad just listened quietly. Finally he said, "Get used to it, kid. You've got 45 more years of this." That brought me down to the ground pretty quickly. Suddenly I didn't feel like such a big deal anymore. I felt like the wind had been knocked out of me.

I don't think he meant to put me down. Frankly, I think he was just commenting on what work was like. He'd been doing it all his life, which was more than long enough to know that the novelty of the office, the desk, and the secretary was going to wear out faster than my first suit.

I've got to hand it to my dad because his words had an enormous effect on me. At that moment I realized that I would be working for someone else for most of my life. And I wasn't happy about it. In fact, that day I vowed that I would become financially independent someday. I didn't want to have to rely on a job to support me for the rest of my life. About a decade later, I discovered investing. And about a decade after that, I realized my dream of financial independence.

Now, most people who achieve financial freedom at an early age either own a business, inherit the money, or get lucky in some other way. Maybe they win the lottery or invent something. I did it by saving and investing, and I did it in a focused, methodical way, which is why I'm able to show you exactly how to succeed.

Knowing what I wanted helped me set up my plan for the future. And luckily for me, I already had something that would turn out to be one of my biggest weapons in my journey to financial independence. It wasn't a trust fund. It wasn't a winning lottery ticket. It wasn't a benefactor or an Ivy League scholarship. It was patience. Patience is the magic ingredient.

I talk a lot about how my street smarts helped set me up for success. But there's more to street smarts than most people realize. It's not just about having the instincts to spot a deal or the boldness to gamble when the odds are good. The really street-smart people understand the importance of patience and caution.

Growing up with cousins and uncles who had street smarts provided me early lessons in gambling and con tactics. When these relatives took me to the track on the weekends and taught me how to play poker, they were always pointing out the tricks and methods gamblers and con men of all kinds used to manipulate people and lure them into handing over their money. One of the most important lessons they instilled in me was that if it seems too quick and easy, something is radically wrong and not to trust it. No matter what, if it's too good to be true, then it isn't true. Period. End of discussion.

Now what does it mean to be suspicious of all things quick and easy? It means you have to learn to see the value in things that are slow and steady. It means you have to learn to be patient. There's that word again.

I'm a very patient man. I don't need to make money quickly. I just need to make it steadily, and I need to keep what I make. I'd already learned not to care about making money fast. I was focused on wanting to have money for the rest of my life.

Right away, this set me apart from many of the people around me who were chasing money in different ways. They didn't understand what I've been telling you, and they fell into many of the traps that I'm teaching you to avoid.

Someone asked me recently why I never got lured into dot-com stocks like so many of my friends. After all, I started investing in the nineties when the market was flying high. Those were the days when an IPO could turn an ordinary guy into a millionaire overnight. Indeed, many investors thought that would happen to them.

I knew that was a pipe dream. The whole setup took me straight back to those weekends at the track with my uncles and cousins. Nothing's that easy. Nothing's that fast. Sure, people get lucky sometimes; everybody has a story about the guy who finds a shortcut to the end of the rainbow and makes off with the pot of gold. And those stories are what pull people into the quick-and-easy scams in droves, only to have them left high and dry.

The dot-com bubble set off all my alarms, which is why I stayed away from those stocks. But most dot-come investors didn't think the way I did. They had what I call an "imaginary millionaire mentality." They weren't millionaires, but they were already planning how to spend their imagined gains.

Back in the day, I knew (and I still know) a lot of people like that. One of my friends used to brag that he spent 90 percent of his money on wine, women, and song. Most of my buddies thought that once they made money, they'd be traveling around in private jets, driving fancy cars, and living like kings for the rest of their lives. Me? I knew that lifestyle wasn't sustainable. Because I was patient, I took the time to crunch the numbers. I quickly saw that you couldn't spend like Warren Buffett unless you actually were Warren Buffett. That's the accountant in me.

And the street-smart side of me knows that being rich doesn't make your food taste any better. It doesn't make people love you any more deeply. And it doesn't get rid of your problems. The truth is, sometimes money gets rid of one problem, but then two more pop up to take its place. Because as hard as you're willing to work for your money, there's always someone willing to work twice as hard to take it away from you.

That's why my goal was always financial freedom with safety. It's not that I didn't want big bucks and big toys just like all of my buddies. But I wanted the security of knowing that whatever I earned wouldn't be taken away from me.

As I've said from the start, I wanted *freedom*. That's what you're about to have too.

My Responsibility to You

Back when I was in kindergarten, I did what most kids did after school. I went to the park and played football. Needless to say, my shoes were always dirty. One day, my mother bought me a pair of expensive saddle shoes. My father pulled me aside to warn me not to get the shoes scuffed. The next day, just as I started to walk home, it began to rain. I took off my shoes and put them in the book bag. I started tiptoeing in my socks all the way home trying to avoid the puddles. My grandmother saw me

— this crazy kid doing ballet leaps in mud-stained socks. But I protected those new shoes.

I did this out of respect for my parents. I had a sense of responsibility to keep their investment in good shape. I feel that same sense of responsibility to you. I want you to know that you should feel confident trusting the advice I'm giving you. Remember, I invest in the same stocks that I recommend to you. And, this is the strategy that enabled me to retire at age 42. I want you to find the same financial freedom that I now have.

PART II

3

UNDERSTAND THE CONCEPTS
BEFORE INVESTING

BEFORE YOU START INVESTING, there is something you must understand first. In spite of what other "investment gurus" might tell you, there is no easy plug-and-play system for investing well and wisely. It simply doesn't exist. There is no way to follow a fictitious set of rules and come out a winner. That's because investing well requires a combination of cumulative knowledge about the market, an understanding of numbers and working the odds, and intuition. And even the best intuition is grounded in years of research and information; you're not simply born with it.

I would never slap some line on a book that says: *Follow Bill's Rules for Making Big Money!* That's baloney. What I can do is encourage you to lean on me to tell you what the best investment opportunities are at the best times. I also believe strongly that an educated consumer is a good consumer, and educating you about some of the philosophies that I follow when I invest will let you understand me better. And the better you understand me and the methodology behind my investment philosophy, the more likely you are to trust me, and by doing so, the more likely you are to change your financial life.

Here are the five most important tenents you should follow:

1. Ignore the stock market chatter.

Let me start you off with a little story that illustrates this principle. When I was eight years old I was precocious — I knew how to get what I wanted, and what I wanted was to go to the football game with my dad. There was a little problem, though. The game was going to start at 8:00 p.m., after my bedtime, and dad said that was too late for me to go. But I was determined.

The backseat of my dad's car had just enough stuff dumped in it for me to crawl under and hide myself. I climbed in, got under a blanket and some other junk stored there, and stayed uncharacteristically quiet. I was going to let him know I was there, but I knew I had to do it at just the right time. If I did it too soon, he'd have to take me back home. But if I waited long enough, he had to keep me. I had to wait until he was about 25 minutes away from the house, because the game started at 8:00, and there was a certain point where he couldn't turn around, drop me back at home, and then make it to the game on time.

So I kept myself hidden back there and when the car pulled out of the driveway, I started to count. From earlier experimentation, I knew about how high I had to count to know we were out of range of the house. I stayed hidden under dad's back seat stuff and counted up to something like 8,000 before I popped up and said, "Hi, Dad!"

Yes, I scared the hell out of him.

Dad was beyond angry, but as I predicted, he had to let me come along to the game. If we turned back around, he'd miss the game and that definitely wasn't happening. Of course, there were no cell phones at the time so when we got there he had to go hunting around for a pay phone so he could call my mother and tell her not to worry about me. We didn't have two cars at the time, so she wasn't about to come and get me. Through analyzing the situation, planning ahead, and figuring out what the odds were that my parents would behave in a certain manner, I got my way.

I was a single-minded and stubborn kid. That's the pigheadedness that has occasionally gotten me in trouble, but has also made me stick to my guns when I know I'm right, particularly about investing. This is the same stubbornness that came up when I wore my bold, red Nike sneakers and everybody laughed at me and said, "Billy, what the hell are you wearing?" I didn't listen to anybody. I did what I wanted to do and what I knew was a good thing to do, no matter what anybody said. Those red Nike sneakers were free and that was a good deal. So I wore them. I didn't listen to anyone's chatter.

Investing requires the same obstinacy. When I first started investing, people immediately started telling me that I was making the wrong moves or it wasn't the right time. It didn't matter what they said. I had made my decision and I was going to get rich as an investor. I didn't pay attention to what they said when they were telling me something I supposedly can't do. The word "can't" simply isn't in my vocabulary. When I set a goal and decided to go after it, anybody who told me not to do it was getting blocked out and I would prove the person wrong.

If you can't block out the chatter, you can't be an investor. It's like being a football player and being scared you're going to get tackled. It's like being a runner and scared you're going to sweat. You're going to get tackled. You're going to sweat. You go into investing and people will try to scare you. People will always be telling you what you can't do, or what you shouldn't have done. You just have to ignore all this noise.

And it goes even further than that. People will comment on the performance of the stock market. Every stock has two different performances. There's the price and the value. When people say,

"Oh, that stock's doing poorly," what they mean is the price of the stock is low. When they say, "That stock's on fire," they mean the price is going up. But what are you investing in when you invest in a company? What makes a company valuable? It's all about *earnings* and what happens to create those earnings.

The market shows us what people think about what a company is doing, but people don't always know what is really happening with a business. What a company does isn't always measurable in the immediate moment. Is the company making money? Is it increasing shareholder value? People don't always know what's going on before a company proves that it is profitable, and a solid stock to own. People frequently react in an illogical way and, as a result, the price of a stock isn't tied to its long-term value. That's why I always say that, in the short-term, the market is a voting machine that measures what people think. But in the long term it's a weighing machine, showing dividends and earnings, according to the great Benjamin Graham, Buffett's mentor.

Let's use a company like Amazon as an example. Its stock rose to $400 per share in December 2013 even though the company wasn't making any profit! Amazon has been online since '95 and went public in '97, but apparently hasn't figured out how to monetize its operations. Of course, most people think Amazon's great, and it is great. People use it all the time. It works perfectly. Instead of driving and paying high gas costs, you log on to Amazon and get almost anything imaginable delivered straight to your door. It gives people a whole new way of life and they think that's the best thing ever. The stock price reflects this enthusiasm when it's going up to $400. It shows the power of the brand. Meanwhile, investors who bought it at $50 and watched it go up to $400 think they did a great job buying that stock. And they were right, but for the wrong reason! Jeff Bezos is a great promoter; Wall Street bought what he was selling and the stock went up. But Amazon as a company does nothing but spend. You go on there and buy a book for 50¢, pay

$3.00 for shipping, and what is Amazon making? It just isn't a profitable business model.

Meanwhile a stock like Apple gets neglected for two years. The stock goes down in value because everybody starts thinking there's something wrong with it. But Apple has more net profit in a quarter than Amazon does in four years! Amazon will never make what Apple does. Just because the stock price goes up people get excited, but the business model hasn't changed. Apple is a good bet. All it does is make money. The stock price goes down, which makes people nervous. They lose track of what Apple's actually doing. It's still making money! So which company are you counting on if you're looking to get back some dividends? It has nothing to do with whether the stock price is going up or down.

Ignore the stock market chatter. Look at the companies. Do the research. Count on the profitable business models, not the high price tags. Study companies like Apple, Altria, and Bank of America. Their stock prices start to go down and people start thinking something's wrong with them. But I've done my research. I know those companies are stable and will stay that way over time. When everyone else is saying not to buy — that's when I jump in and buy.

When I first bought Altria in the 1990s, I told everybody, "Buy this stock — it's got a great dividend." One day someone who worked at one of the big Wall Street brokerages came around and said that Altria was going bust. Some friends had their life savings in it, and this guy basically said that I was going to lose all my money; he said that the company would tank." The other guys were walking out of the room scared to death. But I was just sitting there calmly and a friend asked what I thought about the doomsayer in a suit. I shrugged and said, "Either he's right or I'm right. I think he's full of @#$!" I wasn't investing based on anybody else's advice. I based it on my own instinct and my own research. I knew Altria was a good move. I knew I could count on tobacco. So I had the nerve to stick to my guns. In fact, it is up over 700 percent and, if I had listened to that guy's advice, I would have missed out on one of my greatest investments.

It's tough to tune out what others are saying. You may be a follower — not accustomed to trusting your own instincts. But I say that you simply have to earn your stripes and learn how to ignore the chatter. Trust the real facts, not the gossip.

2. A freatstock has to be bought at the right price.

Warren Buffett likes to say: "Price is what you pay. Value is what you get."

Unfortunately, most people get confused about the difference between price and value. Price is a more obvious concept, and it tricks people into thinking that it is the most important sign of value. You see this in investing all the time. There's something in human nature that makes people love to buy stocks that have just gone up. They don't like buying something that's just dropped. They think if the price goes up, the value has gone up. They think if the price falls, the value must be falling. But often, price and value have nothing to do with each other. Think about a restaurant serving the best cheeseburgers in town for $10. If the eatery kicks the price up to $100, does that make it a better burger? Maybe. You could have the best meal in the world, but at a certain point you're overpaying.

In the 1980s, many Japanese investors came over to New York and bought up some of the greatest properties in the city, such as Rockefeller Center. The problem was they bought at the wrong time — when the prices were sky-high — and they overpaid terribly. The buildings were great properties, but they aren't worth now what they cost back then. These kind of wacky real estate purchases still happen all the time. Somebody recently bought a house in the Hamptons for $147 million. Now, this may really be a remarkable house, but chances are the purchaser will find himself in the same situation as those Japanese investors. When he's ready to sell, he certainly won't be able to get three times the market value that he'll need to break even on his investment.

You don't get the greatest thing in the world on the cheap. You don't get property in Manhattan for pennies on the dollar. The same applies to investing. You have to get the right price. The price is everything. You can have the best company in the world, but if it's overvalued, you won't make any money selling it. A hundred dollar bill is valuable. But would you pay $120 for it? I don't think so.

While Exxon and McDonald's may be great companies, you can't just buy them anytime! You have to buy them at the right time, when the price is right. You have to know when to make that purchase.

Okay, the obvious next question is: How do you know when that is? Well, that's the thing. You need the ability to see quality, or know someone else who does. That means you need to have a way to see the things other people have missed. Take someone like John Getty. He went to an art auction one time and noticed this funny painting that seemed to be ignored by everyone else. He paid $200 for it. He didn't love the painting, but he looked at it and Getty knew it was worth more than the asking price. Nobody else did, but he saw the quality. Most people are too worried about what other people are saying and thinking. They wouldn't buy a piece of art they haven't heard anybody talk about at all. But Getty was looking to invest in quality. He saw that particular work and he put down his money, and it turned out the painting was by one of the greats. It was like one of those true stories when somebody picks up a Rembrandt at a yard sale. Getty paid next to nothing for something that turned out to be worth millions. That was a good buy at a good price at a good time.

I like to think that I have a talent much like Getty's eye. The minute I see something I start sizing up the value. When I go into a store, I can see what's undervalued and overvalued. I was at a thrift store recently when I spotted this big Ohio State football jersey I liked. It was $10, and when I looked it over, it was obvious the stitching alone was worth that much. It was a good deal. I find ways to buy for a penny and sell for a dime or a dollar. I apply these principles not only when I'm investing, but in every area of my life.

Trading baseball cards taught me about perceived value early on. I learned certain ball players were flashes in the pan. There were some guys who were stars locally and everybody wanted their cards, so the price in my neighborhood was high. Now if you could get your hands on one of those cheaply, you could sell it for a good price at the time. But then there were guys like Tom Seaver or Rod Carew who weren't as popular as the local stars, but they were headed for the Hall of Fame. Those cards had real value.

I never lost my taste for baseball cards, even after I grew up. When I was seriously into buying sports memorabilia, my dad and I came across someone who had a bunch of binders full of cards from the '60s — back when I was a kid. I asked him how much he wanted for everything, and he said he wanted $300. Of course, I ran the numbers in my head right away. Three hundred dollars for seven thousand cards meant that I would have to sell the cards for an average for about five cents each to turn a profit. I immediately looked at one of the binders and starting turning the pages. I saw that there were several cards that were worth three or four dollars each. I didn't have time to go through all the rest, but that was okay. I closed the binder and said to my dad, "Give him the money."

Now my dad was thinking that I was taking a big risk putting that much money down when I hadn't looked at the rest of the cards. But from the cards I saw on the first page, I knew that I would make back my money and more. I could sell off some of the cards cheaply and then make more money on the more valuable ones. I kept selling off cards so that I could keep rolling over and increasing my inventory. Eventually, I had more than a million cards in my collection. The last thing I wanted was for the seller to realize that he had individual cards valued at more than he was asking for the whole lot. He obviously needed that $300 and couldn't afford to sit on the potential value of those cards and go through the process of assessing them and selling them off. I could see something was there and I could afford the time to go through and figure out how to get the maximum profit from it.

I quickly bought the cards, and it turned out there were no superstars in those binders. Nothing was worth $200. If you looked at the collection you'd say the cards were pretty much average or even junk. But it didn't matter, because I bought them at the right price. I didn't pay 20¢ a card; I paid 5¢ a card. I was able to sell a bunch of them, make money, and buy some more cards, plus I got to hold back all the cards I wanted. That's what it means to be able to see the value and see that the price is right. I got my money back and then moved on to the next deal. That's how I approach investing; I focus on how fast you can turn your money over.

Now, sometimes you do get burned. Let's say I had paid $160 for those cards and couldn't get more than that amount back. Or maybe I'd turn a few more pages and find that a bunch of the cards were wrinkled or damaged. You're taking chances. But ninety-nine times out of a hundred, I got the value for the right price. There were plenty of times I paid a few hundred dollars for stuff that turned out to be worth several thousand dollars.

It takes instinct and know-how to see the value in different places. If you walk into a designer clothing store and you see a dress that's been worn once and available at a discount and if you recognize the label, you know whether or not the real value is more or less than the current price. Or you can see the details in the sewing and know somebody else would be able to recognize that and pay for it. You can see all the variables: It's a top label, it's been worn once and it's what people like that season or it's not. All that goes into the real value is that the expectation compares to the price. But a person who doesn't pay attention to fashion, or doesn't have an instinct for fashion wouldn't know that stuff.

It's the same with stocks. You have to be able to assess the value of each stock, and it confuses people because they simply don't know what to look for. They don't know anything more than the price tag. A $300 stock might represent a thousand-dollar value, and I won't hesitate to pay for that. But at the same time, I wouldn't pay $30 for Amazon stock because I don't see the value. What do you pay for a company that doesn't make any money? People are sitting around talking about how much Twitter's worth and it hasn't made any money yet! I'm not paying for Twitter stock until I see how the company does over time. I can't see it, and I know from looking at Amazon it could be 10 years before the executives figure it out, if they ever do. Meanwhile, I've got Apple. All Apple does is make money. Price Amazon and Twitter as low as you want, but I'm always going to go pay more for the company I know has the ability to turn a profit.

3. Be greedy when others are fearful and fearful when Oothers are greedy.

The great investors buy when no one else thinks that it's a good idea to buy what they're buying. This is a fact that comes down to the very important difference between real fear and imaginary fear.

When Warren Buffett bought Wells Fargo, everyone else was talking about how business in California was doomed. They thought the whole place was going to crash. Whatever indicators they were looking for at that time didn't matter to Buffett; he knew Wells Fargo had been around since the 1800s and he knew it wasn't going to crumble anytime soon. That was an imaginary fear.

You don't make your money doing what other people are doing. When they get greedy, that's the time for you to be fearful. I had a friend of mine who started buying properties in Florida. Nobody expected him to do it. Nobody else around him was doing it. The idea hadn't occurred to them, or they were scared of making that kind of investment. He wasn't scared, because he'd found some kind of good value at the right price. Next thing you know, he's got a million dollars in his pocket. That got everybody excited! They all started to buy property in Florida. They thought: He did it, so it's a great idea and now I've got to do it. It happens all the time in real estate. The market heats up and people jump in on the trend. In real estate in the 1990s, people started making money and all of a sudden all you heard was buy, buy, buy! But things got too hot, and a lot of people wound up overpaying for property.

Once a trend begins, it's just a matter of time before there's a fall. The people who had the right idea were those who jumped in before anybody else. Once everybody else gets greedy, chances are you've missed prime time, and that value is already in question. When the dot-com bubble was just beginning to inflate, everybody who jumped on those stocks became instant millionaires. Then their neighbors saw them and got jealous. So they bought the same stocks too, but they weren't buying at a low price, as did the people who got in early on.

The time to get the best deals is when people are fearful. Here's a great example: My friend and I used to sell tickets at games and we'd bring ponchos with us in case it looked like it might rain. We'd sell the ponchos we bought at 99¢ for $5.00, no problem. It was threatening to rain and people were worried that they would get drenched. They weren't thinking about the price; they would probably have paid ten bucks for a rain poncho; they feared it would rain so it was a time (for me) to be greedy.

As I said, Warren Buffett bought Wells Fargo when everyone thought the California economy was in bad shape. What about if you live in an apartment building in a big city like New York or Chicago? What are the chances of the apartment building you live in suddenly declining to zero value? There is no chance. But somebody is going to try to shift the market by instilling fear in people. After all, many a dollar is made scaring people. The media loves to scare everybody. But who cares? That hype is just for ratings.

Knowing that is what makes the difference between a professional and an amateur gambler. In the old days in horse racing,
you'd run a not-very-good horse four times and then the odds
would be sixty-to-one. Then the owners would bet on the horse.
One time I went to the track and I said aloud, "I'm going to bet
the four, eight-to-one odds. I think the real odds are six-to-one."
The guy standing next to me says, "I wouldn't bet on that horse."
It turns out he was the owner and knew that the horse I was going
to pick wasn't being run to win; he was only being run to warm
him up for another race. The horse's owner said, "This race is to
get this horse in shape for the next race. If he wins I'll be the most
surprised person in the park."

As predicted, the horse got off to a good start and then faded.
But the next time he went off on twenty-to-one and then won the
race wire to wire. I made the right bet at the right time because I
had information that wasn't available to everybody else. When the
second race came around, everyone else was fearful of the horse,
but it was time for me to become greedy.

That's what I learned about investing. When you buy a stock
you have to do an incredible amount of research. That guy knew
that horse better than everybody. I study every stock for 50 to 100
hours before I buy it.

Hearing something negative about a company or a stock makes
me excited. On the other hand, when I hear something positive
I get scared. When everyone else sees the stock as full value, I
know that I'm not going to make as much money on that investment. The point I'm trying to make is that you have to have an
edge in investing. I'm not talking about illegal information, but
you have to know something that everybody else doesn't know.
George Soros and Bill Ackman are Wall Street billionaires and
were once major JC Penney shareholders, but they didn't know
anyone who shopped there. I was talking to real (not rich) people — the folks who shop at the store. Mothers were telling me
they weren't shopping at JCP anymore because the store wasn't

offering coupons. Soros and Ackman thought JCP was a bargain, but I knew it wasn't coming back. I didn't get fooled; I didn't follow the rich people blindly, because I knew they didn't talk to the housewives.

Someone will start to get uneasy about Apple and offer some criticism. Apple's stock dropped and everyone predicted its demise, but that was an unfounded fear. Everyone was clamoring for Apple products. All I heard about was that the kids love Apple. Parents like Apple. Older people like Apple. Everybody started thinking that there was a problem with the stock, so I started buying it. I knew Apple was a solid company because everyone loved the products, my daughter included. People just like buying stocks that have run up. That's the lazy way to do it. Remember this maxim: What wise people do in the beginning fools do in the end.

Choosing a successful company to invest in is not easy to do, but the basic goal is simple: Go for a company that makes money, not one that has a flashy brand or a trendy reputation such as Cognizant (CTSH), Forest Laboratories (ATC), and Gilead Sciences (GILD). The more money a company makes, the more it can pay its investors, which means the more people will be willing to buy shares. The more money a company makes, the more it can raise its dividend, which makes shareholders want to invest more.

You can't control what everyone else thinks, but you can control what they see; you make money off of stupidity. In most cases, people don't know what they have, so they'll buy something for twenty then sell it for forty, not knowing it's worth several hundred dollars. Doing your homework may be a little time-consuming, but I think that it's pretty simple. If you find this confusing, then you shouldn't be picking stocks on your own. You need to consult with a financial professional — or read my newsletter at 26¢ per day, which, aside from the low price, I guarantee to be a much better value.

4. Don't chase a great stock. be patient and wait for the stock to come to you.

There's a value to every stock. Often people will try to build a position on a stock and the stock price starts increasing. Then the investors get impatient and chase the stock. I told people to buy Visa when the stock was around $70. Now, the stock is around $250. I advised buying it at $70, not the higher price. That's not my investment strategy.

It's the same thing as gambling. At some price, you're overpaying for something. You have to stay disciplined. At a horse race, you could be betting only five bucks, but if you're only winning two bucks, what's the point? The return is not worth the risk of the investment.

Another way to frame it is to think about buying a pair of shoes. If you think these are great shoes and you guess they cost $20 and then get to the register and find out that they actually cost $60, you're basically losing money. Your own perceived value of the shoes is lower than the retail cost. In that scenario, you're not getting anything. You might like those shoes so much you want to spend $60, but in investing, you're putting money in so that you get it back in the future, and if you pay too much, you lose.

Coke was a great stock. But it was selling at 40 times its earning. That means you're putting up $40 to get $1 back. I told my friends to sell their shares of Coke, not buy more. The stock went from $40 to $80 and one guy called my house every day to leave messages as the amount went up. I told him: "Look, dude — this is a fantasy. Coke will never be $80 again. If you bought Coke in 1998, you overpaid. It could be the greatest company in the world, but you're overpaying for it."

When I first started investing in my 20s, there was a stock I liked called TCBY. It was a yogurt company. I bought the original stock. It started running up so I bought more. The day after, it dropped. I lost probably 50 or 60 percent of my money. It ran up and people chased it. And it was dumb. I thought I understood how to invest, but I still didn't understand how to value stocks at the time. I bought it as a speculator, not as an investor. The speculator worries where the stock price is going. The investor worries about the earnings and dividends and how they're increasing. That experience was part of how I built my intuition.

The best investors have a particular approach that may incorporate fundamental analysis or technical analysis. (Don't worry if you don't understand this now.) Most seasoned professionals are accustomed to the vagaries of the market and are able to stick to their strategy regardless of the day to day movements or the "noise" in the financial pages. However, if you're suddenly losing a lot of money in a short period of time, you'll get very nervous and you'll start believing the person on TV screaming at you that you're down! It's very scary, but you must have the discipline to deal with that. Do whatever it takes. You can go meditate or go for a long run. You can even have one drink, but don't overindulge. You have to stick within your investing guidelines. You have to adhere to the standards that make sense according to your age, goals, and portfolio holdings.

5. You can't time the market!

This is probably the most important lesson I want to share with you.

Most people try to time the market. They think the Dow will drop. More precisely, they feel the Dow will drop. Who cares?

When I invest, I know. I don't just *feel*, and I don't just think. I feel and think. Before I put my money down I don't say "I think . . ." If you got on a plane and the pilot said, "I think I can land this plane safely," you would immediately get off the damn plane, right? Okay, so what does that have to do with timing markets?

When you're an investor, timing is all noise. The trader thinks he can jump in and jump out at the right time. But it's impossible to know the "right" time. You shouldn't try to time markets. You want to pick a stock and figure out its value. If you're a frugal shopper like me, you always look to buy quality things at a cheap price. You don't wait for the sales after Christmas. When you see something at the right price, you buy it. Nine times out of 10 you've made a smart purchase. Sure, you may get a bargain when you buy an item on sale, but you don't *know* for certain. Investing is about getting your money in an investment that is the right one for you.

There's a saying: Sell in May and go away. Some years that works. Some years that's the dumbest thing you could do. There's no way to tell; even the Icahns and Buffetts and other billionaires can't time markets. What they *can* do is find a good stock at a good price or a decent stock at a very good price. And then they just sit there and they wait. No person has ever become a billionaire by being a sector rotator.

Some people rotate from one sector to the next. They buy utilities and then jump to housing and continue to switch from industry to industry. That's not smart investing, in my book. You have to find your niche and learn everything about it. You can't just say that you want to buy housing stocks. Each stock is its own market. Don't time the market. Just buy an individual stock when it is under the price that makes the most sense.

In 2011 the stock market dropped precipitously. The S&P 500 dropped 22 percent from August to October. Many people predicted the drop off would continue, but in fact, the stock market didn't drop. It did nothing but run straight up. In the fall of 2011, the S&P was 1076, and it went straight up at the record-setting rate of 1995 in late summer 2014. One man told me that he was waiting for the market to pull back before he put his money there. He told me this in January 2012. Well, there hasn't been a market pullback. There have been slight pullbacks, but it's gone up. You can't time the market. This investor has been sitting there in cash not making any profits and he's missed the biggest bull market in recent history.

I'll say it again. You don't time markets. You buy individual companies. Each stock is its own market. You choose a particular stock that you want to own without focusing on whether it's been going down or up. You want to buy it when it's a good deal. You want to layer down. As it drops in price, you buy a little more and you know that you're getting a good deal.

What does "layer down" mean? Move on to the next chapter and find out.

Wringing More Value Out of Stocks

When I'm picking stocks, I look for those that will provide me with more value than meets the eye. It's a good sign when a company regularly pays dividends and also raises them.

I developed this concept of finding value while enjoying one of my favorite pastimes. Back in the 1980s, my pals and I frequently went to Cleveland Indian baseball games. We would bring pizza from Little Caesars to the games. The other fans were jealous because only hot dogs or Cracker Jacks were available at the stadium. We ended up selling slices of pizza to people for two dollars each. That wasn't cheap, but no one complained because we were the only ones with pizza! At the end of the night, my buddies and I had watched a game, had dinner, and made enough money to cover the cost of the tickets and parking.

Layering Down and Other Key Strategies

BEFORE I EXPLAIN LAYERING down and the rest of my strategies, let me share some of my tactics for finding the best stocks.

Observe "Insider Buying"

I've already talked a lot about how having an edge can happen in various ways. It could be that you know numbers like I do. It could be that you've got information that no one else does. It could just be that you've spent more time doing research on your stocks than anyone else. When you've got many different areas in which you've got an edge, you're golden.

Remember that horse I was warned not to bet on? Those were the days when trainers and owners — guys like Joe the Hat — would use their advantage to work the system. They weren't supposed to bet on their own horses, so they had other people place the bets for them with bookies. The number of people betting affects how much you can win, so getting your bet in at the last minute could sway things in your direction, giving you an edge. Back then, when you had a hot tip, of course you wanted to collect, but not so much that the bookies would catch on, and definitely not at the track, or you would throw off the odds and ruin your payday. This type of betting was Joe the Hat's edge, and the key to some of his success.

Joe the Hat also had an edge with regard to betting on football games. He was able to get the NFL's confidential injury report each Friday. Today this information is public knowledge and available every Friday, but in the 1970s, it wasn't available to the general public. Joe the Hat had this edge. I don't how he got it, but it gave him a pretty good idea of how the games were likely to turn out based on which players were going to get on the field and which ones wouldn't have a good day. With the horses, Joe the Hat's advantage was that he knew how to play the numbers. With football, it was all about getting insider information. Joe the Hat had it covered. He did very well for himself; he had this edge — and I use the same principle in my newsletter, *The Dividend Machine*.

Applying this analogy to the stock market, having the NFL injury report is comparable to what's known as "insider buying." As I've said endless times already, whenever you're making any kind of investment, you're looking for your edge. Insider buying is all about getting and holding on to available information that *you're* looking at, but other people may not be. Or if they are, they're not getting the whole picture. For me, if people such as Carl Icahn, Leon Cooperman, and David Tepper — three of my favorite, self-made, multi-billionaires — all move in the same direction toward a stock, I know I'm onto something. In other words, if you're paying attention to the right people in the right way, you've got an edge. You're looking at what highly successful people who are inside the business of investing in a very serious way are doing; and then you act on it. If the insiders buy a particular way, you may want to consider watching them and doing your own "insider buying."

Insider Buying Is Not Insider Trading

Most people have heard of "insider trading." Even if you have no experience in investing or the market and have never looked at *The Wall Street Journal*, chances are you've heard this phrase. Remember when the domestic diva, Martha Stewart was convicted? Anyway, she went to jail because she got caught up in insider trading.

Insider trading is when people act on information that's not public. Let's say you work at a company that is planning a merger, but word of the merger isn't known outside of the company. You cannot act on that information if it's not publicly known. There is a world of difference between having an edge and having an unfair advantage, particularly one that allows you to buy or sell your stock and then wind up affecting all the other investors' holdings and dividends. You have to play fair or you could wind up in a lot of trouble.

Don't Follow the Whales Blindly

These wildly successful investors — those whom others tend to watch in order to make their own decisions — are called whales. These multi-billionaires are investors who own large stakes (five percent or more) in companies or really big hedge funds. If you're a whale, you have to go public and state that you have a five percent position. This means that everyone else gets to see the holdings of these very rich people. You can find out who owns your stocks, what they're doing with them, and decide if you want to follow them or not. You see, that's a vital piece of information. YOU decide what you do with your stock, not the whale. Why is that? The whales are really just people who are right a lot of the time, even most of the time, but not all the time. Sometimes they're just flat-out wrong. Warren Buffett bought ConocoPhillips. I had followed him into five or six stocks, but I didn't follow him into that one. I just didn't see anything good happening and I stopped. It's a good thing I did because the stock went down. Similarly, George Soros bought JC Penney and *it* went down. No matter how many times the whales win, remember: They're not always right.

Still, in the past, when a big respected whale has followed me into an investment, I've never lost any money. When you make a pick and you've got the big four investors following you, it's like having four brain surgeons looking at the same patient. The chance of all four being wrong and making the same mistake is extraordinarily low. So if you've got the team of brain surgeons on your side, you're getting an edge. When I bought AIG, four or five big hedge funds bought in at the same time I did. The fund managers were all seeing the same thing I was. That kind of thing makes you more comfortable about your investments. MUCH more comfortable!

Never forget this, because it's true in investing and in life: You can't just follow people blindly. Sometimes I follow other investors, and sometimes they follow me. Carl Icahn followed me into Apple (AAPLE) and Transocean (RIG) and I followed him into Nuance (NUAN) and Herbalife (HLF). And we both wound up doing very well.

Why Layering Down is Important

To be a smart investor, you need to understand numbers, have an edge, understand who the whales are, and why you sometimes want to follow them.

"Layering down" is another way to be smart and careful. I've said it before, I'll say it now, and I'll say it again: Make your investments boring and your life exciting, not the other way around! Layering down means that when you buy a stock you don't just throw all your money in at once. Let's say you have $40,000 that you're prepared to invest in a company. First, put in $10,000. If the stock drops, you buy a little bit more. If it runs up real fast, you don't chase it. So you layer down. Layering down means that you build up your investment like you would a layer cake. You don't just dump all the ingredients in a bowl, stir them, throw it in the oven and pull out a perfect chocolate layer cake, right? No, you build it up; you bake the cake layers, you frost the first one, then the next layer, and so on. You get my drift? Layering down is putting your money into a stock in installments (think of each one as a layer in the cake!) so that you wind up with the right amount invested, but carefully and in pieces. The whole is greater than the sum of its parts for your investment, just like your cake. Get it?

Why should you layer down? What kind of an investor are you? Are you a smart investor who has a long-term view or a speculator who wants a quick return? Another big difference between the investor and the speculator is that the speculator makes a lot of different bets on stocks, and if the stock runs in one direction, he or she jumps off the train. Investors keep that long view.

Warren Buffett is one of the greatest investors of all time. He's got vision. He made his greatest investment in the Washington Post. He bought the stock and then the stock dropped in price by half. Multiple stocks he bought dropped in half right after he bought them. He didn't care! The difference between the pro and the amateur is that the pro loves when stocks move around like that. What goes down will eventually come up (for the sake of argument, let's use that as a rule of thumb). And the pro doesn't give a damn about what anyone else is doing or saying; he or she knows the numbers, has the intuition, and has the research down cold. Buffett's second-in-command, Charlie Munger once said, "Just because other people agree or disagree with you does not make you right or wrong. The only thing that matters is the correctness of your analysis and judgment." Amen.

Okay, so we know an expert layers down. But what does that look like? If I buy a stock at $10, and it drops to $8, I buy more. If it drops to $6, I buy more. If it goes back to $10, I just made a 25 percent. That's not bad. Not only did I not risk all my money right out of the gate, but, by waiting, I got consecutively better deals with each layer of my stock purchases.

The pros have the confidence and tenacity to just sit there while the market fluctuates. They have conviction. How do they know they're right and everyone else is wrong? The reason the experts (including myself) can sit tight is because they are not afraid — analysis and experience tells them they're right. I liked Bank of America stock at $13 and I bought it all the way down to $6. Everyone kept asking whether I was afraid that the price would go down to zero. I wasn't afraid because I knew the tangible book value was about $14. Most laymen wouldn't understand that. The fear was that all the banks would go broke. But I knew that the banking system doesn't work without the four biggest banks in the country, including Bank of America.

There are stocks I layer down on that have literally no chance of going to zero. With some stocks, I'm not as aggressive about layering down. There aren't set rules and I approach each company on its own merits. The difference between the pros and the amateurs is that the professional, experienced investor is happy when her stock goes down because she knows she can buy more of it at a cheaper price. The speculator is upset because he's trying to predict the market.

As I said, the people with knowledge and conviction like to buy stocks down. But even they don't always buy every stock down. In my conservative portfolio, it WILL get bought down. In my aggressive portfolio, it MAY get bought down. This is where instinct comes in. I wish I had a more precise system that I could share with you. Markets fluctuate in unison with many other variables that only the seasoned investor can recognize. This book is intended to get you to begin thinking like an investor. In my newsletter, *The Dividend Machine*, I teach you my theory as you simultaneously put my advice on stock picks and portfolio building into practice — sort of like on-the-job training. Once you've gotten plenty of experience under your belt and you're able to trust your own judgment, the training wheels come off and you'll be well on your way to achieving what I have.

Here's another good analogy for what I'm talking about. I was going to bet on a game one time. The team, I liked, was a four-point underdog. As the week went on, everyone was betting the favorite. In gambling what happens is you bet a team, but the gamblers want to even the money out. They don't want everyone to bet on one side. The four-point underdog might end up a seven-point underdog, often to force people to bet the other side. So if you like the team to lose by four or less, you've got to love the team to lose at seven points.

Why Reinvesting Dividends Is So Powerful

Out of everything I do, this is the most magical. The power of reinvested dividends works like this: you buy a stock and you get a dividend. You put your money in and the company sends you a check every three months. It's that simple. If you take that money and waste it on the latest toys or taking a trip, that's your choice. But, if you take that money and reinvest it, it's a whole other ball game. Reinvesting the dividends is simply an extremely powerful investing strategy.

For instance, consider Visa (V). We paid $73 back in 2010. Now it's priced at more than $250 and pays a really low dividend. When you reinvest a dividend, it's not a lot of money. The reinvested dividend helps, but remember: It's still just a very small percentage. With Altria (MO) we paid $16 for the stock, but it paid a very high dividend of about $1.28 (back then) and now $2.04. When you reinvest that dividend, you're buying the shares back at something like $18 or $19. (They are now are over $45 a share.) But, you're getting a significant number of those shares. The dividends are high; and if you keep reinvesting those, they grow exponentially.

As far as I'm concerned, the most powerful force in the universe is compound interest and the reinvesting of the dividends. I've seen what I'm talking about. Let's say you own Altria stock. Let's say you have a hundred shares. Your dividend comes in and you can buy two more shares. Now you have a hundred and two shares. Now your dividend is higher because you have two more shares. Now you can get two and a half shares. Now you have 104 and one-half shares. *Over time, your shares are more powerful because you've got more of that money working for you.* On the other hand, if you own Visa, the amount of the dividend might only buy a quarter of a share. But for the person with Altria, the compounding is enormous. Take a look:

> If you had invested in $10,000 in Altria in 1957, and reinvested all the dividends the company paid out from 1957 to 2014, your initial investment would now be worth well over $160 million. *That's an enormous amount of money and shows that the power of compounding is huge.* But it takes a while for that much money to accumulate in your portfolio. Like anything else, time changes everything. The longer you hold the stock, the longer the compounding happens.

Here's a great story: There was a woman in the Midwest who invested $180 in one stock about 70 years ago. She did it one time only with one stock, and because of compounding, she just reinvested the dividends into the same company. Instead of taking the profit she just kept it running. When she died, her stock was worth *seven million dollars*! When you see that sort of real-life example, it shows that even with a modest investment of less than two hundred bucks, you can build a future for yourself and your family that is limitless. That's the premise of *The Dividend Machine*.

Who Is Using the Power of Compounding to Get Rich?

People think you need a lot of money, but in the story I just shared with you, the woman had less than $200 to invest. While it's true that most of you won't become rich in one generation, you can still take steps to boost your wealth. What if that woman had a daughter who did the exact same thing? This woman would have started a family tradition that in only two generations would create enormous wealth and stability for many future generations of her family.

If you want to provide financial support for your grandchildren, don't buy them an iPod. Buy them a share of Apple (AAPL). By giving them an investment, you're providing a three-pronged lesson. First, you're teaching them about a product and what's behind it. And, if you talk with them about your investment, you can help them understand how what they buy comes from a larger corporation which uses the money from selling shares to continue to create nifty products, which in turn adds to the value of the corporation. Instead of giving them macaroni and cheese, get them a share of Kraft (KRFT). And listen to your kids! I'll bet many kids under age 12 understand Apple, its branding, and its products better than you do. My daughter explained Apple culture to me. She said, "Everybody knows that you need more than one case for your iPhone — having only one case is like wearing the same purse with every outfit." That would not have occurred to me in a million years, but it could very well be a great tip.

The bottom line is that even if you don't want to invest in stocks or become financially secure, show the power of compounding to your children. I showed the son of a friend about the power of compounding. He's not even 20 years old and is hoping to retire before age 30! He's presently working toward that goal, and I can't wait to see what happens to him 15 years from now.

Some of you are thinking: Show me the money . . . How much have you made with dividend reinvesting? I have personally averaged 18 percent each year over the past 21 years. If you compound your money at 18 percent annually, a one-time $10,000 investment will grow to $5.2 million in 36 years. Can you see why one person can retire in 40 years and the other person can't?

You just had a baby. Congratulations. Take $2,000 and invest it for your new offspring. By making this one-time investment, and assuming you earn compounded interest at 18 percent, you will have accumulated $80 million when your child reaches age 66. Let's say you wait and then put aside $4,000 in a Roth IRA when your child is between14 and 18 years old, compounded at 18 percent, your child will have some four to five million dollars when he or she reaches age 50. This is the difference between the rich and the poor. I never made a lot of money. Rich people compound their money and hang onto it. You have to save to get rich and save to stay rich.

I know a millionaire who's afraid to buy stocks. He had a bad experience back in the 1990s when he was investing very aggressively, and he's been spooked ever since. I can't even convince him to use my conservative approach. So, even though he's got a lot of money, he's behaving like an amateur; he allowed that bad experience to frighten him into complacency. The amateur cares what he's going to *make*; the professional looks at how much money he *can lose*. The professional thinks about what would be the worst thing to happen in the stock market.

To finish first, you must first finish. A psychiatrist, considering investing with me, asked me many questions. I must have passed the test because after about an hour he said that he would invest with me. What convinced him were two exceptional traits that he said I had. Firstly, he said that I was totally oblivious to whatever anyone else thought about me. Secondly, I move away from things, not toward them, as most people do. This trait means that I'm not like most investors who are focusing on making the big kill. I will steer you away from stocks that would cause you to lose money. I invert everything. I look at a situation and ask myself: What's the worst thing that can happen, and can I live with it? Most people say they only have a 30 percent chance of losing, so they'll invest. I say to them: Would you jump out of a plane if you had a 30 percent chance your parachute wouldn't open? By my insistence on inverting the commonly held view, I'm a safe and successful investor.

The concept of "buy and hold" is more than a one-time investment credo. It's a lifetime commitment to a particular kind of behavior. The people who maintain a sizeable weight loss for years and years have committed to a new lifestyle. They eat differently and they exercise. But most people end up as yo-yo dieters because they never commit to changing their behavior. If you don't want to keep investing and losing, and hope for that financial stability you crave, you've got to make a lifestyle change. *The Dividend Machine* is that lifestyle change in a ready-made package.

Finding That Winning Strategy

The Dividend Machine is a proven strategy that has helped thousands of people over the past 20 years. It's a tried and true method. It may not be sexy, but adhering to this framework is guaranteed to provide financial security.

I've always had a knack for problem solving and strategizing. When I played baseball as a kid, I had a really low batting average — around .140. You wouldn't think that any team would want me playing, but I had a secret weapon: my on-base percentage. A good on-base percentage in the major leagues is around .330, meaning a player is getting on base about one third of the times he gets up to bat. Obviously, you want to get on base because that's how you score. My on-base percentage was .500! I calculated that unless the ball was perfect, my chances of getting on base with a walk were higher than getting a hit.

5

DON'T SWING FOR THE FENCES

INVESTING ISN'T FOR THE faint of heart. I've been knocked down so many times, and I keep getting back up. That's just my nature. But it's served me well because each year, I keep getting it right and my percentages improve. My ability to take the pain of making mistakes in the past has given me the education I need. I've gotten to the point where I can invert everything now. My confidence is grounded, and for a good reason. I know what to gravitate toward and what to stay away from. Let me ask you this: If you had one wish and you couldn't wish for more wishes, what would you wish? I know right away. You'd want to know the place where you will die. Why? Simple — so you don't go there. What does that have to do with investing? *Everything*.

What frustrates people most is when they try to do something and they're continually met with the same obstacle. Many people get caught up in trying to fit a square peg into a round hole instead of striving for balance. I've managed to achieve this balance in life; for instance, one way I've done so is by positioning myself in a location where I'm 10 minutes from downtown Cleveland and a 30-minute drive from a remote spot where I can't even get cell phone service. I'm lucky enough that I can move between those worlds when I need to focus in a different way. Many urban dwellers think they can't survive unless they're in a crowded city, but if they could get out of their urban jungles, they would acquire a fresh perspective on the world. What's more, most people go through life compelled to live up to the expectations of others — to "keep up with the Joneses," when the Joneses can't even keep up with the Joneses!

I may boast about my successful investment techniques, but I'm also quick to admit that I can't invest the way rich people do. I didn't do so when I first started buying stocks and I still don't today. The biggest mistake in investing that most of you make is saying that you only have $10,000, so you'll gamble with that money. You might go out and hire an advisor, although you would probably find it difficult to select and then vet the so-called "professional." Or you might subscribe to some other financial newsletter. Now, I've admitted that I've gambled in the past, but you don't want to gamble with your hard-earned money. And listening to the guy in the next cubicle isn't going to get you far. About half the time, a stock is just going to go down, so you'll end up frustrated and losing money.

Really, I don't mean to sound egotistical, but if you follow my strategy, your chances of losing over a long period of time are almost non-existent. For some 40 years I've honed a system that is virtually fail-proof. *The Dividend Machine* succeeds, and that's what brings you power.

The little guy can't swing for the fences. That's why I'm conservative. Other investment or financial planning newsletter writers don't average big numbers. They go for what's flashy and splashy to keep people interested. I don't care if I'm boring at first because you'll be much more interested in my methodology when you've seen your first dividends come in. And then I'm even more fascinating when you follow my advice and reinvest those dividends. Numbers are what's exciting. Flashy is fun for the moment; conservative investing is much more fun in the long run. And I can back my statements up: I've delivered 23 out of 23 conservative selections.

The bar is set low for investment newsletters; I've been approached by others and was asked to be right 60 percent of the time, which is really being wrong 40 percent of the time. And I said, "What about the people who buy the stocks that go down 40 percent of the time?" THAT is the fundamental difference between *The Dividend Machine* and any other advice you'll get. I know that I can't afford to be wrong 40 percent of the time with my money, so why should I ask you to be wrong 40 percent of the time with yours?

Remember the psychiatrist who questioned my mindset before investing with me? He told me I had a high threshold for pain, and he didn't mean physical pain. He said, "You couldn't care less whether somebody agrees with you." It's not about whether people think I'm right or wrong. It's whether I am actually right or wrong. And my record shows I'm right!

I'm focused on protecting your assets. What's going to stop you is not that you run out of money, but that you run out of guts. What happens to people's momentum? The world kicks them in the stomach and they say, "Forget it, I give up." I don't run out of steam because I already know how the stocks I pick behave, and if there's a hiccup I'll get right back on track with an alternative strategy. I focus on picks that won't triple or quadruple in two months, but that are not going to lose money and not going to fail.

Most people don't have a high threshold for mental pain like I do. That's okay, because when you follow my methodology, you don't need to have nerves of steel. How you handle adversity is how your life invariably goes. When you get knocked down in life, there are three things you can do: quit, complain, or get back to work.

Bust Those Myths

Most people take for granted that investing isn't a stable endeavor; they think that by virtue of its fluctuating nature, it can't be. I completely disagree with that view. When done correctly, it can be a very stable prospect. And once again, the right way is by taking advantage of dividends.

Think about my dividend machine as being an actual, physical machine. What you put in, if the machine is running properly, will consistently put out the same thing. When you went to the automat, you put in a quarter, turned the window, and got a ham and cheese sandwich every time. Your dividend machine can be every bit as reliable. But it won't quadruple your money in two weeks. That's not real. That's a fantasy — it doesn't happen in real life.

In the movies, investing has become incredibly sexy. Think *The Wolf of Wall Street, Margin Call,* or *Arbitrage*. People get excited about the idea of investing because of the projected possibility of fast and huge returns. Sorry, folks — we all watched Superman, but we didn't come out of the theaters able to fly. Investing is business . . . it is the business of making and losing money. Riding on a roller coaster is exciting. But the problem with riding a roller coaster is that it always ends on the bottom. The best investing is boring.

Let me stick with the movie analogy for a minute longer. Some people love to invest in films. They can walk the red carpet and they can rub elbows with celebrities. They briefly get a taste of a life they normally only look at from the outside. They're not putting money into the film expecting to get a great return on their investment. They're buying access to the industry and a brief thrill. In fact, the mindset of the movie investor is actually the proper mindset of the financial investor. If you want to have the excitement of gambling or blowing your money on risky stocks, know that you're blowing your money and that what you're really doing is buying a sexy experience. That's okay if you've got money to burn, but I know that most of you don't want to do that.

I'm a big believer in trusting your gut; throughout this book you've been reading about instinct. Ralph Waldo Emerson wrote: "A foolish consistency is the hobgoblin of little minds, adored by little statesmen and philosophers and divines." On the other hand, when you're investing, consistency is not a hobgoblin at all; it's your best friend. Carl Icahn averages 30 percent a year on his money. He's been doing it for 35 years. He doesn't double or triple his money — he stays right around 30 percent. Warren Buffett can't double or triple his money either. He earns 22 percent a year, but he's been doing it for 50 years consistently. Everyone would love to say that they tripled their money. It won't happen in six months, and if people say they've done it, run the other way because they're scammers.

Without going into a detailed analysis of this fact, let me just remind you of Bernie Madoff and the Beardstown Ladies. Well, if you've somehow missed the news, Madoff is serving a 150 year sentence for carrying out the largest financial fraud in American history and the Beardstown Ladies Investment Club was sued when its annual profits were far less than it touted in several best-selling books. In investing, as in life, when something looks too good to be true, it is. Investing is a long-term endeavor. Setting realistic goals is essential if you're going to stay the course. It will keep you from being discouraged when your life doesn't change overnight.

Instinct comes from the school of hard knocks for everyone. The best lessons you learn come from your mistakes. Money and life overlap; you can't separate who you are from what you do. People who run hedge funds do it because they are interested in making huge amounts of money. They have the drive and the instinct to go in for the kill. Whether they're right or wrong about their picks is another story.

Looking for Someone You Can Trust

This book isn't meant to teach you how to be a master investor. What I want to show you is how to select and trust a master advisor. How do you pick a good advisor, and what makes me different from other people?

First of all, look at the advisor's *track record*. Bill Parcells, the famous football coach, said that you are what your record is. The legendary investors I've been referencing have been doing it for 45 or 50 years. They're not flukes. Be wary of investment advisors whose job is to bring in clients, not to make the clients' money. Those people have no track record. You can find an advisor at some of the larger financial institutions like JP Morgan, Wells Fargo, or Merrill Lynch. The problem is that advisors at these companies are supposed to preserve your money, not grow it. They might want to grow it, but they're not personally invested in how much money they make for you. They get paid a percentage of what they manage. So they don't care if they make you eight percent, three percent . . . whatever. If they're making two percent for their management services, and they get a two million dollar account, they're paid $40,000 to manage your account and not lose it. They're not going to take any chances. And if they're not taking chances, what are you paying two percent for? You could do that yourself.

Second, you should ask: Do they have dividend income themselves? How can someone who doesn't earn dividend income have the necessary information to tell someone else how to retire? People can't retire because they don't have enough income to replace their salaries. Your job is to develop your dividend machine. The path to a retirement nest egg leads back to buy and hold, like the lady who bought the one share for $180. All she did was tell her advisor, "Reinvest the dividends, please." Your advisor must have dividend income for you to work with him or her. Would you hire a gardener who's never planted before? Most investment advisors, in my view, just aren't focused on dividend investing.

I know someone whose advisor told him to buy a muni bond yielding two percent rather than investing in Apple. Apple is up more than 80 percent since then. What's ironic is that the advisor told him: "You own more Apple stocks than any of my other clients!" I told my friend that the advisor wasn't making money from recommending Apple stock.

The people managing your money at a big firm aren't geniuses. If they were, they'd have their own hedge fund. If you have five million dollars, you can have a hedge fund. But if you don't have big money, your investment money gets put in a mutual fund, mingling with a lot of other people's money. You're not getting personalized attention. Investing anything less than a million dollars only gets you that. And the people doing the investing for you are making two percent. The people running the fund don't take any chances because if they lose money, people will withdraw their money. When you're a private investor you don't care about the short-term, you care about five years from now.

Why Fundamentals Trump Technical Analysis

What does this mean? It's actually really simple. "Fundamentals" is the raw data about any company — its value, the price of the stock, its history, etc. When you're looking at the fundamentals, you're looking at everything you need to know to make your own decision about a company without anyone else having interpreted the information for you. You're looking at what has happened with a certain company so far and then using that information to project what it could do in the future. On the other hand, "technical analysis" means that some entity (a bank, a broker, a hedge fund manager, for example) has taken the raw data and processed it into a chart that can be read more easily in one glance than all the raw data. But the charts are still someone's interpretation of raw data that is static. That document is not a live, evolving document. It simply reports what has happened to date. It's already been digested and is being regurgitated back at you with the analyst's bias attached to it.

To me, chart people are those who don't have the brains to understand the fundamentals. They don't have the numbers and accounting background. Using a chart to predict the direction of a stock is like driving forward while looking in the rearview mirror instead of looking ahead — it doesn't make sense. Looking at a chart only tells you what the stock has done in the past, but it doesn't tell you what it can or will do. Chart people think the chart is telling you what a stock is going to do. It doesn't. It can, sometimes. But it doesn't *all* the time. Just like driving, sometimes you need to look in the rearview mirror, but mostly you look ahead.

A stock is worth a percentage of its future earnings, but we all know that the future is always uncertain. People say, "I'm waiting for the future to become clear." When will that happen? Even intelligent people are delusional. Everyone's delusional about something. I'm just lucky that I'm not delusional about investing — I know that it's 50 percent science and numbers, and 50 percent art and instinct. When I buy a stock, I need to see the numbers and I need to have that instinct to make the decision.

There's a playoff system that I use for stocks. The system ranks the top five stocks. I start with number five against number four, and I play them against each other. The winner moves on. What happens then is that I take the stocks and discuss them with a panel of people who don't know each other and all work in different industries. I tell them to make a case against the stock and I'll make a case for buying it. We go head to head. If someone can crack my argument on the stock, I'm done. The stock doesn't move on. And then I keep playing the system. Finally, I take the two best possibilities and play them against each other. Sometimes both make it and I play them both, but usually one stock comes out ahead. And that stock goes either into conservative or aggressive play.

Why You Need both Conservative and Aggressive Holdings

Conservative stocks will account for 90 percent of your portfolio, and 10 percent will be comprised of aggressive stocks. Conservative stocks have no chance of losing money over a 10-year period. But they're not going to do anything exciting. Aggressive stocks have a chance of quadrupling, but you have a 30 percent chance that you'll lose your investment.

Here's an illustration of why we work this way: Years back, a buddy and I did a favor for someone and in turn, he gave us a good tip on a horse. I can't remember if he owned the horse or knew the guy who did, but back then we trusted him. We went to the track and saw that the horse was going to race at four-to-one. We both had five hundred bucks with us. The horse wasn't running until 5:30 p.m., so there were many races we could bet on before that particular one. Unfortunately, we lost every race. My friend lost $400, or 80 percent of his money; however, I only lost $50 — 10 percent of my money. I bet the remaining $450 on the 5:30 race, and got back $1,800. We both started with the same amount of money, but I knew how to manage mine. That's why you put 90 percent of your money in conservative stocks and only 10 percent in risky stocks. I left the track with $1800 profit. My friend left with the same $500 he started with. Choosing to bet (or invest) conservatively or aggressively is all about money management.

How did I first get the idea to manage money this way? When I was a kid I read a book about gambling called *Picking Winners*. The author explained how he split his bets at the track: he separates his gambling into "action" bets and "prime" bets. The prime bets are the ones about which the guy feels really strongly — he bets that money on three horses he really loves. Then he'll put that 10 percent of his portfolio on the action bets — the horses he has no opinion about. Your big bets have to go on your most confident picks, but the action bets satisfy the need for excitement.

It's the same with stocks. You can't bet big. You have to bet small. If you have $100,000, you can risk $10,000 — you can't risk $50,000. If you have $10,000, you can't bet it all on an aggressive stock. You could tap out and lose all your money. But on the conservative bets, you won't.

No one wants to be around someone who's boring. I don't say don't gamble — I say learn how to bet. When you do, this system will maximize your profits. But it's like a diet — you won't stick to a diet that is very restrictive. Everyone has to know their limitations. I'm at the stage where I know what I'm doing because I have all the elements necessary to make good decisions and trades. But you don't. And there's no reason you should. What I do for you, through *The Dividend Machine* newsletter, is take that decision-making process out of the equation for you.

Consider this: An investment of $10,000 in the S&P 500 index at its 1926 inception with all dividends reinvested would have grown to approximately $33,100,000 (10.4 percent compounded) by the end of September 2007. If dividends had not been reinvested, the value of that investment would have been just over $1.2 million (6.1 percent compounded) — an amazing gap of nearly $32 million. Over the past 81 years, then, reinvested dividend income accounted for approximately 95 percent of the compound, long-term return earned by the companies in the S&P 500.

The purpose of this book is to draw a line in the sand on the issue of investing. It shouldn't be difficult for the average person to make the market work for them. Most people in the financial advising business make investing confusing on purpose. They want you to think they're performing some sort of magic that you're unable to perform yourself. They can't tell you that it's easier to just subscribe to *The Dividend Machine*. If they did, they'd be out of work in about five minutes. You can pay a broker a big fee, you can sweat it and do it yourself without any training, or you can have me do it for you at 6¢ an hour by following my newsletter. That's a no-brainer.

Go for the Big Idea

When you get a good idea in investing, you have to bet big. This is a great quote from American business magnate Charlie Munger: "It's not given to human beings to have such talent that they can just know everything about everything all the time. But it is given to human beings who work hard at it — who look and sift the world for a mispriced bet — that they can occasionally find one."

When you get a good idea, go with it. Three investments in my life have made me 98 percent of my wealth. I had the chutzpah to bet big on all three of them. Not surprisingly, they're all dividend-machine stocks. Altria (MO) is the best stock I have. I recently told everyone to buy as much Apple (AAPL) as they could. The third is Bank of America (BAC). You have to bet big. Use buckets, not thimbles. Don't hide under the bed. When you feel the odds are in your favor, you have to bet big. However, you can't bet big on everything. You can only do so much with what you've got. But, this is the funny thing: People say, "I have limited capital." Guess what? Warren Buffett has limited capital too. He's just playing on a different scale. Everyone has limited capital. Everyone has one 168 hours in a week. Some people can't get anything done. Other people get everything done. You have to learn how to manage it.

This is a self-help book of sorts. But the problem with self-help books is that readers think they're going to transform their lives once they finish reading the books. While you may be able to make some changes, it's unlikely that you'll truly alter yourself. I'm going to teach you a great deal about picking stocks. But do you have 50 or 100 hours to study the markets? And, even if you had the time, it would still take you years to acquire experience doing so. What I can do is share my knowledge and experience of the markets. If you're really smart, you'll let me do the work for you. I'm the guy who's been in that jungle for many years and who knows how to fight for you. I'm not telling you how to be like me; I'm telling you why you should trust me.

Protecting Your Money, Not Swinging for the Fences

I was a wrestler in high school. During the first match, I spent all my energy trying to shoot in on my opponent, and pretty soon, I was on my back and lost 9 to 7. But If I waited and wrestled defensively, I would capitalize off my opponents' mistakes and win. I learned not to risk getting reversed or flipped on my back, and it must have been boring to watch me. But I didn't care because that strategy allowed me to win six straight matches after being a second stringer during my first two years of wrestling. This is a difficult concept to teach investors, but you have to protect your investments to come out ahead. This strategy — like my wrestling philosophy — it's not exciting, but it works.

PART III

THE DIVIDEND MACHINE AND **HOW IT WORKS**

NOW LET'S GET STARTED on *The Dividend Machine.* If it's going to help you to have the financial freedom, stability, and potential to create the life that you want, you need to become familiar with it and how to use it.

Take a look at the following quotes. These are a few of my favorite quotes about dividends, and they should illustrate exactly why smart investors should focus on dividends, above and beyond anything else. If you're not sure what a dividend is, don't worry. Here's the down and dirty definition: the word "dividend" is from the same Latin root that gives us the word "divide." Dividends are the profits of a company in which you've invested — they have been divided up and paid out to you and the other investors. That's it, plain and simple. I bet you thought it was a lot more involved. It's not. Financial savvy can be yours if you get out of your own way. Here are those inspirational quotes that speak to the power of dividends:

"Do you know the only thing that gives me pleasure? It's to see my dividends coming in."   — *John D. Rockefelle*r

"I don't like stock buybacks. I think if a company has the money to buy their stock back, then they should take that and increase the dividends. Send it back to the stockholder. Let them invest their money again from the dividends."
— *T. Boone Pickens*

"I believe non-dividend stocks aren't much more than baseball cards. They are worth what you can convince someone to pay for it."   — *Mark Cuban*

"A stock dividend is something tangible — it's not an earnings projection; it's something solid, in hand. A stock dividend is a true return on the investment. Everything else is hope and speculation."   — *Richard Russell*

These experts knew or know what they're doing and all agree that money talks and everything else walks. And dividends are money.

Okay, so let me be perfectly frank about the internal workings of *The Dividend Machine*. Like all machines, it's got a lot of moving parts. Some of those parts involve straightforward math, but math that is most likely out of the average person's league . . . and interest! Who wants to become a math whiz if it isn't absolutely necessary? I'm betting you don't! Know-how is an integral component, which only comes from years of being an investor and making both good and bad choices. Some of the components are based on extensive research about dividend-paying companies and their CEOs. That's research that goes back many years and has to be maintained every day. Even if you read the financial pages of your local paper, you probably don't have that amount of research at your fingertips. Finally, there's the weirdo, x-factor part of the machine, which is the casing that holds it all together. That's me — I'm the x-factor. The way I look at the world, as I've already shown you, comes from a very particular mix of experiences and natural inclinations on my part.

All of this is to say that, unlike many other financial investment gurus, I am not going to give you complicated advice and send you on your way to succeed or fail. I'm going to do the hard work. I'm going to give you very explicit instructions about what you should do *every single week*. You'll get those instructions in *The Dividend Machine* newsletter. The directions are simple and easy to follow, so you'll have no excuse not to do what I tell you.

What I want to share with you here is a peek behind my strategy. I'm really showing you how I approach investing. I want you to understand that I'm not selling you a bill of goods and that my way of looking at investing has real grounding and truth. My track record isn't the result of good luck and it isn't the result of people with good luck following my advice. It comes from adhering to all of the principles I've already discussed in this book. Following this approach has helped me and thousands of others have more freedom than was ever thought possible.

The Ten Principles of *The Great American Dividend Machine* and Why They Work

1. Be consistent.

I have dubbed my system *The Great American Dividend Machine* because once you implement it, you essentially have the potential to grab the American dream via your own personal ATM that spits out cash on a regular basis — cash that is yours simply by owning the stocks I recommend.

You won't have a million dollars in your bank account by Friday. But by focusing on these concepts for 15 minutes a day, in just seven days, you will have a blueprint for achieving all of your financial goals.

2. Focus on buying dividend-paying stocks.

I call these stocks "warhorse stocks" because they are typically mature companies with established businesses. Most importantly, they have proven that they can survive and thrive in the worst of times. I'm talking about well-known names, like Coca-Cola (KO), McDonald's (MCD), Intel (INTC), and Microsoft (MSFT).

These are companies that have a long history of consistently paying dividends every quarter, year in and year out. Coca-Cola, for example, has paid a dividend every year since 1920. McDonald's has paid a dividend every year since 1976.

Think about what that means. Many of these are companies that have been able to meet their obligation to return a portion of their profits to shareholders even through the Great Depression, the 25 percent unemployment rates of 1932, the 18 percent interest rates of the 1970s, and the financial collapse of 2008 and 2009. These businesses aren't going away at the first sign of difficulty. That's the kind of safety I'm looking for, and that's why having a long history of paying dividends is the first screening tool I use in selecting a stock.

3. Find the right stocks.

Find stocks that have consistently increased their dividends year after year. I examine the businesses to determine what factors will be moving these companies in the future. I look at how the businesses are run along with the products or services they're providing. This research is designed so I can then put a price tag on every company that I'm considering buying. This enables me to see whether a stock price is over or undervalued.

4. Take advantage of the power of compounding.

Albert Einstein referred to compounding interest as "the greatest mathematical discovery of all time." This is why I stress the fact that reinvesting your dividends as part of your investing system will allow you to turbocharge your returns. If you continue to do this year after year, you will have compounded your returns dramatically, because you are not only realizing appreciation and dividends on your initial investments, but also appreciation and dividends on your appreciation and dividends!

When clients come to me for my accounting services, one of the first things I look at is their cash flow. How much money do they have coming in and how much do they have going out? It's pretty basic, right? Obviously, the more money coming in and the less going out, the better off they are. And the more cash they have on hand, the better. The same is true with the stocks I invest in.

One of the things I like about companies like Microsoft (MSFT), Apple (AAPL), and Old Republic International (ORI) is that they are sitting on a ton of cash.

Microsoft has more than $68 billion in cash. Apple is sitting on $137 billion in cash, and Old Republic has nearly $10 billion in cash.

This shows me that these companies have enough of a stockpile to maintain their dividends. Of course, a storehouse of cash also gives these companies the ability to invest in new products if they want to acquire new business or even whole companies.

5. Look at debt.

When individuals are spending a large percentage of their income — or worse than that, they owe more than they make — I'm concerned. I take the same view with the companies I evaluate. There is a statistic called the "current ratio." This is basically a company's current assets divided by its current liabilities. Heavy debt is not a good sign. I am even happier when a company has little or no debt. Apple (AAPL), Marvell (MRVL), and Visa (V), for example, have no debt at all.

Of course, there are many variables, and there are plenty of good reasons that companies take on debt, like investing in other companies or growing certain parts of their businesses. If the company's debt is at a reasonable level, it doesn't represent a large percentage of market cap, and the cash flow is available to pay it down, then this debt is acceptable.

A company that isn't saddled with debt is similar to an individual being free of debt — the people and the companies have much more freedom to spend or invest their cash as they see fit. And these are often the companies that either buy back their own shares or return their cash flow to investors in the form of dividends. The current financial ratio shows how easy it is for the company to pay back its short-term debt; the higher the ratio, the better. For example, if a company's current assets total $200 million and its current short-term debt is $100 million, its current ratio is 2. It has twice as much cash (and inventory and receivables) as it needs to pay its current obligations. This is what I like to see.

6. Look at future growth potential.

I want to see future earnings growth potential, too. Microsoft (MSFT) is on a similar steady growth path. The computer software giant had EPS (earnings per share) of $2.55 as of December 2015, but it is forecast to have EPS of $2.85 for 2015 and $3.49 for 2016.

7. Understand perceived value.

Value is an interesting thing. We like to think that we are smart enough to assess whether something has intrinsic value or not. For example, we assume that a $175 bottle of wine tastes better than a seven-dollar bottle of wine. Or that a $16 million baseball player is more valuable to a team than a $500,000 one. Both assumptions are often wrong.

Michael Young's salary for the Texas Rangers in 2012 was $16 million. But, with 651 at bats, Young only managed to get 169 hits and eight home runs. Young's cost to the Rangers: two million per homer. Andrew McCutchen, on the other hand, earned just $500,000 from the Pittsburgh Pirates in 2012. Yet he managed to score 31 home runs on 673 at bats, making his cost per home run a meager $16,129. On top of that, McCutchen finished the 2012 season with 194 hits, making him the leading hitter in the National League. Which player is the better investment? McCutchen is, of course. Not surprisingly, his salary ballooned to $4.5 million after that strong season.

Value is subjective. It often isn't fully realized by the market, because the market frequently gets distracted by other variables such as a brand name, but some people who pay up for a brand name like Coach or Tiffany learn that the brand has little to do with an investment's real value.

Similar to the Pittsburgh Pirates, we can snag bargain investments that are worth far more than what the market currently values them at if we know how to evaluate them objectively. One way to do that is by looking at the price-to-earnings ratio (P/E ratio). The P/E ratio is the price of the stock divided by its earnings per share; the lower the ratio, the better. It means either the earnings are high relative to the price of the stock, or the price of the stock is low compared to its earnings. Either way, it's a good indicator that a stock is undervalued.

But as with EPS, I don't look only at the current or trailing P/E ratio. Again, doing that is like driving a car and trying to figure out your destination by looking in the rearview mirror. You have to look ahead. So I look at the forward P/E ratio as well.

A stock like Marvell (MRVL) has a current P/E ratio of 16.2, but a forward P/E ratio of 13.12. But I don't stop there. This ratio means little by itself. You have to compare it to other stocks in the industry, as some industries just by their nature grow faster than others.

In Marvell's case, the industry average is 22. Since Marvell is trading well below the average, it's a good sign. That's one reason this stock is on my buy list.

Looking at the P/E ratio sounds simple, but the number is actually complex and is really a function of growth. A large company will not typically grow nearly as fast as a smaller one. Chipotle, for example, has more room to grow than McDonald's because it is newer, can expand to more locations, etc. Because of this, fast-growing companies tend to have higher P/E ratios. Chipotle's P/E ratio is 35, while McDonald's P/E ratio is 17.

8. Buy stocks when they are priced low and sell when they are priced high.

You've probably heard this before, but then the obvious question becomes: When is a stock priced low, and when is it high?

You see, even solid companies aren't great investments if you buy them at the wrong price. You know this intuitively. If you overpay for anything, whether it's a washing machine or a smartphone, you feel cheated.

But in investing, the consequences can be even more dire — they could seriously eat into your nest egg. And if you are like most investors, you will then make even more dangerous decisions, trying to chase returns to make up for the mistake of buying at the top. It's a never-ending cycle.

The only way to make money is buying low and selling high. Don't make the mistake of thinking that a good stock will make you money no matter what. It won't if you overpay for it.

9. Investing is an art form.

Successful investing involves more than just comparing the statistics of one company to another. It is as much an art as it is a science. Part of that art lies in understanding that each company has its own key indicators of financial health. And those indicators differ from company to company. In a way, I look at each company as its own market. I get to know what has propelled the company forward in the past and what has caused it to lag.

For example, a key indicator for Altria is its market share on Marlboro cigarettes. For Coca-Cola, it is about how many 12-ounce servings the company sells.

In more than two decades of investing and nearly 30 years of studying accounting and tax planning, I have discovered that these key indicators can often be the tipping point between an average year and a stellar one for a business.

A lot of this is an art and takes some experience to interpret, but you can get started simply by following the company's news. The easiest way to do that is to set up a free Google Alert. You can sign up at Google to receive e-mail notification whenever a company is mentioned in the news.

The numbers always grab the headlines. Are earnings up or down? Is the stock price up or down? What is the P/E ratio, the PEG ratio (price/earnings to growth), the return on assets, the price to book value — the list goes on and on. As I've said, these numbers can certainly be important indicators. But they can also mask the importance of management, which is also crucial to a company's success.

Remember, when you buy stocks, you are investing in businesses. Those businesses may be in a growing industry. They may have a great product. They may even own the lion's share of the market. But if management isn't top-notch, those businesses won't realize their full potential — and in the worst-case scenario, they can get in serious trouble.

General Electric (GE) is a great example of this. From 1981 to 2001 under CEO Jack Welch, GE thrived. His focus was on streamlining the company, famously saying that GE had to be either number one or number two in any industry it was doing business in or the company would get out of that business. But since Jeff Immelt took over as CEO of GE in 2001, the stock has dropped 63 percent due to what many claim is a lack of vision on Immelt's part (and I am inclined to agree).

The flip side is even more important. If management is exceptional, even a seemingly horrible business can be turned around. I have seen this happen time and time again. One of my favorite examples is American International Group (AIG).

AIG was, of course, beaten to a pulp in the financial crisis of 2008. From a high of $42 a share in March of 2008 to 33¢ a share by March 2009, AIG was in such bad shape that many thought the giant insurer would never recover. After all, the company had been the recipient of the largest government bailout in US history.

But when tough-talking, Brooklyn-born Robert Benmosche took over as CEO after the crisis, everything changed. Jim Millstein was the restructuring officer hired by the Treasury Department to work with AIG. In a recent *Barron's* magazine article, Millstein said of Benmosche, "He was the right combination of bull in the china shop and crazy like a fox." It's a skill that has served AIG well. AIG has nearly paid back all of the bailout money, and its stock is on the rise. CEO Benmosche used his tough reputation and can-do attitude to get risks under control and the government repaid. To do this, he needed to reduce AIG's footprint. He wound down the financial products unit and put everything up for sale.

Other great CEOs include Larry Ellison of Oracle Corporation and Tim Cook of Apple. They have the skills and instincts to drive their companies forward. Not surprisingly, these stocks are also on my buy list.

As I've said many times, investing is 50 percent science (the numbers) and 50 percent art (instinct). CEO evaluation is a large part of that art. John Paulson became a billionaire by shorting the subprime mortgage market in 2007. Hedge fund manager David Einhorn made a similar call with Lehman Brothers in July of 2007 and again in October of 2011 with Green Mountain Coffee Roasters (GMCR), which subsequently plunged over 35 percent in a month.

Do you think it would have made sense to follow the advice of these successful hedge fund managers back then? Of course it would have. If the biggest, richest, and most successful investors are buying a stock, why shouldn't the little guy get in on the action? Wouldn't that be a simple and smart way to invest?

As for the portfolios of mortgage-backed securities and collateralized debt obligations, which were collateral for the Fed's loans to AIG, they were auctioned off by the Federal Reserve. Now those loans are paid, and as prices have risen, the Fed made money, and AIG recovered some of its losses.

I watched AIG closely for over three years before recommending it. I liked what I saw Benmosche doing, but I wanted to see him make greater strides to financial solvency. AIG hit my sweet spot in December of 2012, when the price was low enough to still be a great bargain, but the company was then sound enough to have limited risk.

10. Pay attention to the cat.

Consider this: In 2012, a cat beat a group of professional investment managers by throwing a toy mouse on a grid to pick stocks. The cat racked up an 11 percent gain, while the pros turned in just four percent, according to London's *Observer*.

Yes, even the big guys (those so-called "whales" that the financial press loves to follow) get it wrong sometimes.

Billionaire Ray Dalio and his firm, Bridgewater Associates, manage the largest hedge fund in the United States. Yet in 2012, a year when the S&P gained 13 percent, Dalio's flagship fund was up just 0.8 percent.

And after consistently beating the S&P 500 for 15 straight years through 2005, Legg Mason's Bill Miller then promptly underperformed the market for the next four years straight.

Clearly, whale watching doesn't guarantee gains. There are many reasons for this. For one, whales, like all investors, know certain industries better than others. Warren Buffett, for instance, is much better at choosing financial stocks than he is at picking oil companies, airlines, or technology firms. Another reason is that the 13F forms that the whales file with the SEC are reporting what these investors have already bought. If you're buying after the forms become public, chances are the whales got in at a much better price. And if the whale is a trader, like David Tepper or John Paulson, he may already be out of the stock by the time the 13F form becomes public.

Now, whale watching is a part of my investment approach, but not in the way most people view it. I don't look at what the whales are buying and follow their picks. I do the opposite. I evaluate stocks using my own proprietary system. But if a whale happens to be buying one of the stocks I'm evaluating, I take note of it. If the whale has had success in that industry or sector, I consider it a good sign. For example, when I recommended AIG, I did so after watching the stock for more than three years. During that time, I also noticed that legendary investor George Soros had bought more than 15 million shares of the stock. And hedge fund managers David Tepper, Leon Cooperman, and Daniel Loeb also had big stakes in the beleaguered insurer. These are guys who have had success investing in financials.

When they moved in, it was definitely a vote of confidence for my move.

Now, I never choose a stock based on what someone else does. But when my formula and the whales agree, that bodes well for us. You won't be able to find out what the whales are buying now, but you can get an idea of what they have bought in the last quarter. It isn't something I think about consciously when I select a stock. But if some of the greatest investment minds on the planet are following what I'm doing, I'm pleased. I'm never going to recommend trading like some of the big whales do. When little fish swim in big ponds, they can get eaten, after all.

The good news is we don't have to. We can enjoy plenty of sleep-well-at-night, market-beating gains simply by doing what we're already doing: buying quality, dividend-paying stocks that consistently beat the market over time.

One More Time, It's all about the Dividends

These are some of the many factors that go into my proprietary, stock-screening system. They form not only the basis for my stock-screening methodology, but also my philosophy about investing in general.

Trying to time the market is like trying to bet against the house in a casino. You may win one or two hands, but the house will always beat you over the long-term. Instead, we make the choices that are proven to stack the odds in our favor. Study after study proves that dividend investing provides the best long-term results. Study after study proves that stocks with increasing dividends provide superior returns. And study after study proves that reinvesting dividends compounds your returns exponentially. That is how you beat 90 percent of investors out there, including many of the big hedge fund managers and traders.

If you don't want the x-factor that will push you over the top as a successful and independent investor, you can go it alone. Using this basic blueprint that lays out my philosophy and credos, you'll do just fine. Or you can let me help. There's no reason you have to spend all that time on research yourself. Let me do the legwork for you.

How *The Dividend Machine* was Born

I never wanted to be like everyone else. I just never wanted to have a nine-to-five job. I started investing in real estate, but I soon realized that it was too capital intensive. Five thousand dollars was not enough for me to really invest in real estate, and the interest rate on borrowing money was 13 percent back then. With a stock, you pay once and then every three months you get a dividend check. With a piece of property, you have constant expenses like maintenance, interest, and taxes, along with the stress of worrying whether your tenants will pay the rent on time. I learned that I could borrow on margin with stocks, and so my dividend strategy was created.

Making *The Dividend Machine* Your Own

I'VE TAUGHT YOU ALL the basics about finance, investing and how to value what's in front of you (not to mention within yourself). I started this book by telling you the absolute truth: You can't be me. You can't wake up tomorrow with all the experience, street smarts, book smarts, aptitude, gut instinct, and tenacity that I've got. But, what you can do is follow my lead.

I promise you that this investment strategy will change your life and future generations of your family. There are three simple steps to getting started:

1. You will need to raise about $2,000. If you don't have this money available, following my money-saving tips in the appendix following this chapter will help you raise it. If you've already cut all the fat from your budget, you may

need to borrow the money. (For tips on borrowing, see my suggestions on the next page.)

2. Open a trading account with an online investment site. There are numerous companies that provide roughly the same services, like Ameritrade and E*trade. Whichever you choose should charge the lowest possible percentage as a service fee.

3. Subscribe to *The Dividend Machine* and follow my instructions for six months. That's a relatively short period of time, but it's long enough for you to see the proof that this strategy really works. And when you get your own proof that this strategy really works, you'll be ready to change your life. Don't forget: Like this book, my newsletter comes with a 90-day, money-back guarantee. If you don't recoup the cost of the subscription by using the strategies I teach you, you will get a full refund.

A Few More Details
Raising Start-Up Capital

You should have at least $2,000 to begin building your dividend machine. Hopefully, you have this money, but if you don't, and you've already distilled your budged down to the bare minimum and applied my money-saving tips offered in appendix I, I urge you to borrow it. Ask your parents, grandparents, friends . . . whomever. Say that you'll pay two percent interest, which is more than anyone's bank is paying. You see, the interest you'll earn from the stocks will be higher than the two percent you'd pay a willing friend or family member to borrow it. And the interest you'll be paying would be way less than on a bank loan. Your quarterly dividends will help you pay off the loan. Or instead, maybe you have to borrow $50 from 40 people. But if you want to secure your future badly enough, you'll find a way to come up with the money. Let's face it, if you can't raise this modest sum of money, you'll never become wealthy or have a secure future.

Why *The Dividend Machine* Always Works

Because of the way my dividend machine runs, neither you nor I will ever wake up without a dollar. When you buy a stock that's the *right kind* of stock, you can just sit back and relax. You will get a check every three months. You can take it in cash or reinvest it, but you will get to see the dividends. Receiving this money isn't costing you anything. Investing in stocks, according to my principles, is incredibly easy and stress-free.

We are investing conservatively in stocks that cannot go to zero. If you go to a casino and make a bet and lose, you lose all your money. With my strategy, there is no losing. Conservative investing isn't sexy, but it sure is dependable.

Being Right All the Time with Conservative Stocks

An advisor may pitch you a particular investment and say that he makes the right picks 60 percent of the time. Chances are you're paying this advisor a two percent brokerage fee, along with other fees. Being right 60 percent of the time isn't enough for me. I'm right all the time with my conservative stock picks. So far, I've been right on 23 of my 23 conservative picks. Eleven of the 23 stocks — almost half — are up 80 percent or more. Seventeen of 23 picks are up 49 percent or more, with the four best choices up 277 percent, 49 percent, 156 percent, and 152 percent, respectively. When you buy the stocks I pick, you get a check every three months and you can reinvest the dividend and keep building a portfolio of stocks.

A recent survey from TIAA-CREF showed that 65 percent of people don't want financial advice. However, of the people who get financial advice, 86 percent act on it; 62 percent will spend less money; 56 percent will save every month; and 46 percent will increase the amount they save for their retirement.

But why would you want to pay some advisor a hefty fee to be right some of the time, when you can pay me 6¢ an hour to spend a full week finding these stocks for you, as well as teaching you how I did it. I am also offering a 90-day, money-back guarantee for my newsletter and for this book. For less than $2.50 per week, you will get a weekly newsletter, a podcast, and a monthly report. If you want to read testimonials from satisfied subscribers, go to appendix III, or to DividendMachineReviews.com. There you will find video testimonials as well as a welcome video.

Well, at this point, I hope I was able to make good on my promise to EDUCATE, MOTIVATE, and ENTERTAIN. I also hope you take my advice, and that you can get your children interested in building a secure future and managing their money. Why not give them a copy of this book to get started? I'm offering you sound advice and a money-back guarantee. You and your loved ones have nothing to lose.

Appendix I:
Prioritizing and Saving

So now you may be thinking: I'm ready to subscribe to *The Dividend Machine* newsletter, but I simply don't have the start-up cash to begin building a portfolio. That may be the case now, but by following my advice and implementing the following, simple, money-saving tactics, you can easily free up the capital that you need to begin investing in your future and the future of your family. Read on to find out how.

Setting Priorities

To get started on the road to transforming your financial reality and generally prepare yourself to become the person you know you'd like to be, you've got to set priorities. You can't have or do everything. No one can. So you've got to pick and choose what's important to you and what's right for you. Anything else will be a distraction. Setting or not setting priorities will make or break you. Nobody has an infinite amount of money or resources. This fact guides you in everything you do in your life, so don't forget it.

As I see it, the main priority we all have is to be able to live the way we want as quickly as possible. In order to achieve the lifestyle that you desire, the two variables that must be present are time and money. You've got to have the time to enjoy your money, right? So, in other words, your priority should be to retire. Let's face it — the options are not vast. You have two choices: work your whole life or retire quickly. If you start a dividend machine at 14 and you get on a 25-year plan of working and contributing to it, at 39 you're done. And by "done" I mean done working. No more answering to anyone else. Most people are done at age 70 or 80. What's the point of that? What are you going to do then? Chances are you won't really be able to enjoy surfing when you're 80. Focusing on retiring early allows you to enjoy life when you can enjoy it the most.

When I knew I had to set priorities in order to make my life better, saving money became my number one obsession. I didn't have some crazy scheme; I did what most people would do. I cut out little expenditures, which wound up adding up. This is stuff you can do as well, if you're not too proud to live lean now in order live fat later. So, for example, if I was hungry, I'd eat free samples at the mall. Cutting soda out of my diet saved me a hundred grand. Don't believe me? Do the math yourself. How many bottles or cans of soda do you drink a week? What about the rest of your family? Now multiply that by 52 weeks. That two- or three-dollar drink that seems like nothing adds up, doesn't it? People laugh at me when I go out for dinner and I don't order a drink, but that's who I am. It's not that I can't afford it. I just went so long without it that now I don't want or need it anymore. What was a cost-cutting necessity became an ongoing lifestyle choice that benefits me in many ways to this day.

What I'm saying is accept that you can't do it all. You have to choose. You have to pick your goals and stick with the program you put together to make them happen. It can be something as small as not buying drinks or as big as downsizing your home or driving a cheaper car. Ask yourself: What's really important to me? What do I *need* and what do I *want*? And be honest with yourself about the difference.

The idea that you can live the American dream and have it all is way out of date. It just doesn't work that way anymore. People think they should be able to do it all because their grandparents did. But it's a different world! Your grandfather didn't have any debt, or at least not the kind of debt people now have, with huge credit card balances or mortgages they can't afford. Your grandfather was probably an immigrant, worked incredibly hard and had very little money to spare for anything. But he had something else — *chutzpah*, or gall bigger than the Empire State Building. He was unafraid. He had nothing to lose, so he had the luxury to be bold enough to go for broke. Every immigrant population has the same focus when it comes to this country: Save more than you spend. That's it. And surprise — it worked. You need to have more money coming in than going out. That's the difference between the time that the American dream was born and now. Today, we all live far above our means and think it's normal; however, it's only normal if you want to keep working until you're dead and leave behind a pile of debt.

There's a simple formula for saving money successfully. When you get paid, immediately take 10 percent of your earnings (after taxes), put it in a savings account, and never, ever touch it. That's it. You don't have to think about this again. If you feel you can't live without that 10 percent, then look at how you're spending and make the necessary changes. Try to have three to six months of living expenses in the bank in savings. That's your safety net. I'm going to say this again: You need to save at least 10 percent of your income and never touch it. I give this advice to everyone, regardless of their background, whether single, married, or unemployed. Stash the money. Forget it exists. Never touch it — EVER.

People want to believe that accumulating wealth is more complicated. They want some system. While there are various strategies to use to boost your savings, they all revolve around common sense moves. Think about it. If you go to the doctor with a pulled muscle, she can order all kinds of tests and X-rays that will cost you (and your insurer) a lot of money. Or, she can tell you to take two aspirin every four hours, ice it, and if it still hurts in a few days, call her. The latter is a simple answer to a straightforward problem. Would you really need all those tests? I don't think so. So why are you looking for a complicated answer on how to get control of your money and your life?

Are you familiar with the concept of Occam's razor? Here's the idea: If you've got a problem to solve and there are a bunch of ways to do it, choose the simplest way. Why? Because it has the least variables, and the more variables a solution has, the more opportunities there are for things to go wrong and your problem to go unsolved. The complicated ideas or theories *could* work, but the safest bet is with the simplest solution.

As I've stressed, it's not about having the money to spend, it's about having the money so you don't have to worry and you can do exactly what you want to do every day of the rest of your life. With that goal in mind, you need to make some smart choices. You can continue to spend wildly, buying the latest gadgets and handing over your credit card every time your children ask for something from the mall. Or, you can start living comfortably, but well within your means today so that you have the freedom to do what you want in the future.

Here are my best, tried and true, money-saving tips:

1. Take advantage of low mortgage rates.

If you haven't refinanced already, consider it now before rates move higher, advises Tom Reddin, former CEO of LendingTree.com and publisher of MortgageRates.us. "In this low-interest-rate environment, many homeowners will be able to refinance with minimal costs," he says. "You can opt for a 'no points' refinance, with expenses limited to required items such as a documentation fee from your lender, attorney fees, and title insurance as your main expenses."

Reddin recommends getting four to five offers from various lenders, then examining the interest rates and all the fees side by side.

Savings: Paying one percent less by refinancing a $200,000 loan would lower your payment by about $125 per month, freeing up $1,500 per year for other uses.

2. Get your title insurance reissued.

As you refinance, ask your lender for a "reissuance" of your title insurance from the same insurance company that currently underwrites the policy. "This can save you hundreds of dollars versus working with a new insurance company," Reddin says.

Savings: Depending on the amount of insurance involved, you'll save $300 to $500.

3. Shave four years off rour mortgage.

"A really fast and easy way to shave four years off your mortgage is to ask your lender to set up automatic payments from your bank account every two weeks instead of once a month," Reddin says. "This can reduce a 30-year mortgage by more than four years." How? Because of the math involved, you essentially end up making 13 monthly payments instead of 12 every year.

Reddin recommends making it automatic rather than depending on yourself to send in a payment every two weeks because, well, we're all human. Most people won't have the discipline to stick with it long-term, he points out.

Savings: Four years of interest payments on your mortgage loan. For a $200,000 mortgage, our sample family might save between $20,000 and $30,000 over the life of the loan.

4. Get a new quote for your life insurance policy.

Many people have had life insurance for years and probably don't even know the policy's value. Chances are you're carrying too much or too little coverage.

Savings: Get a free quote for new coverage from SelectQuote.com

5. Update your car insurance.

Unless you have to file a claim, you may not be familiar with your automobile coverage. But you can save substantially depending on a number of factors from whether your children use your car, the yearly mileage, type of model, whether you've taken defensive driving courses, etc.

Savings: Get a free quote from esurance.com

6. Rethink your heat/air-conditioning system.

Adjusting your thermostat by seven to 10 degrees for just eight hours a day can save up to 10 percent in annual energy costs. You can get a programmable air thermostat in most hardware or home repair stores. Also, make sure your air conditioners' filters are clean so the units run efficiently.

Savings: Conserving energy this way saves $15 per month on a bill of $150 per month, or $180 per year.

7. Reset your hot water heater, or install a solar model.

Lower the setting on your hot water heater from 145 degrees to 120 degrees — the only place you'll notice the difference is on your utility bill. And depending on where you live, you could save as much as 50 percent on the cost of a solar water heater courtesy of tax credits and grants at federal, state, and local levels.

Savings: Resetting your hot water heater's temperature will save up to $61 per year. Potentially, a solar-powered heater can save up to $800 a year.

8. Replace your shower head.

A new 2.5 gallon-per-minute, water-efficient shower head — coupled with taking showers of 10 minutes or less — will use five fewer gallons of water each shower, as well as less energy to heat the water.

You should also repair any leaky faucets around the house. Those drips add up — hot water leaking at a rate of one drip per second can waste up to 1,661 gallons of water annually, as well as the electricity or natural gas it takes to heat the water.

Savings: With average shower use by a family of four, a new head can save up to $145 a year. On average, repairing a leaky faucet can save $35 a year.

9. Get rebates for replacing appliances.

Utility companies often offer rebates in order to encourage consumers to replace energy-gobbling appliances with energy-saving ones. Check with your utility companies to see current offerings, as well as with the Database of State Incentives for Renewables and Efficiency (dsireusa.org) to find out what's available in your area.

In addition, search online to see whether the manufacturer offers a discount coupon or rebate, and check with the store where you're making your purchase, as well.

Savings: Depending on what appliances you buy, you can save anywhere from $250 to $750.

10. Swap skills.

Are you great with a paintbrush but hopeless when it comes to completing even the smallest electrical task? Instead of paying an electrician, see whether you can find someone who knows how to repair what you need fixed. By placing ads for prospective trades on local website bulletin boards, you can probably find someone who's willing to trade labor.

Savings: While rates vary depending on your locality, electricians can charge $40 an hour or more, so swapping services for a three-hour task such as installing track lighting over a kitchen island would save you $120.

11. Pay upfront.

Paying the entire car or home insurance premium upfront instead of paying in quarterly or monthly payments will pare down the cost. Several insurance companies including Progressive, Safeco, and Travelers offer savings of 10 percent or more for paying in one or two payments a year. Making automatic payments from a credit card or bank account can also get you additional savings.

Savings: A 10 percent discount trims $90 a year off car insurance. The Ohio Insurance Institute says the US average homeowner's premium is $968. Slicing off 10 percent would save our family $96 on home insurance premiums.

12. Consider a health savings account.

Carrie McLean, senior manager of customer service at eHealthInsurance.com and one of a handful of people in the country licensed to sell insurance in all 50 states, suggests families consider enrolling in an HSA-eligible health insurance plan and opening a health savings account, especially if they're not frequent users of healthcare.

"HSAs can only be used with qualifying high-deductible health plans, but they allow you to save money on a tax-advantaged basis for future medical costs," she says.

Money not used in one year will roll over to the next and can earn interest tax-free. "The contribution limit for HSAs in 2013 is $6,450 for family coverage; adults aged 55 to 64 can contribute an extra $1,000 per year," McLean says.

People find HSAs confusing, but essentially they are the same as taking a high deductible on your auto policy. With these policies, if your car is totaled, the carrier is there. But if you dent a fender, you're responsible for repairs. The same applies to the HSA-eligible plan. Depending on your deductible, you are on the hook for between $1,500 and up to $10,000 a year of health costs (doctors, drugs, whatever it might be, at 100 percent with no copays), but you are covered 100 percent after hitting the annual limit and, typically, have no coinsurance and no cap on coverage.

The higher deductible, the lower your premium.

Essentially, you trade a sure loss ($10,000 to $12,000 in premiums every single year) for a potential loss (the one-off cost of a big problem, such as a major accident and hospital stay or, say, cancer treatment). If your medical costs are minimal to none, you can keep that money in your HSA and roll it over, earning interest in the process.

Savings: Insuring a family these days on your own costs $13,375 in premiums with a typical HMO, while an HSA plan with a $10,000 deductible runs $3,696. So the savings in one year is $9,679. Even subtracting a few doctor visits and perhaps some simple prescriptions, the typical family could bank a significant sum, which should be socked into the HSA account for future healthcare costs. The total does not count the family's tax savings from reducing their taxable income by $6,150 off the top.

13. Ditch your bottle habit.

If everyone in a family of four drinks the recommended eight, eight-ounce glasses of water per day, at 16 ounces per bottle, that would be 16 bottles daily. At eight dollars or more for a case of 24 bottles, that's close to $2,000 a year — for something you could be getting out of the tap for much, much less. If you're concerned about taste or purity, you can buy a filter for your faucet or a pitcher with a built-in filter.

Savings: Of course, our example might be considered a little extreme for those who aren't big water drinkers, but you can see how reliance on bottled water can add up quickly. For a family who drinks a lot of bottled water, you could figure approximately $1,500 a year in savings by switching to tap or filtered options.

14. Get a head start on next season.

Look at the end-of-season sales as the time to make your purchases for the following year. So when it's winter clearance time, mentally frame your purchases as getting ahead on next year's cold season. You can often save up to 75 percent on winter items, and remember, down coats and boots don't usually go out of style.

Fred Brock, author of *Live Well on Less Than You Think*, adds that even retailers with high-quality clothing (think L.L. Bean or Lands' End) have end-of-season promotions. "You can save a lot of money on clothes if you buy them off-season or really watch for sales," he says.

Savings: For a family of four, if you can get just a quarter of your family's clothes purchases at steep discounts, you could save roughly $500 a year.

15. Call for cheaper cell bills.

A family spending $300 each month on a cellphone plan needs to shop around for better deals, which come out all the time in this competitive market.

"Stay updated on what your cellphone company is offering, even if you've been a customer for a while. I just did this, and they were able to drop our bill by $40," says Lori Mackey, a financial literacy expert and founder of the Los Angeles-based company Prosperity4Kids, which teaches money-management principles to children.

Also, go online and see whether you can drop features from your package you're not using. This tactic can yield an easy 10 to 15 percent savings ($540 a year).

In addition, if you're not under contract with a provider and, say, T-Mobile coverage is good in your area, head to Wal-Mart — the superstore often offers unlimited talk/text/data deals, through well-known providers starting at about $50 for the first line and $30 for each line thereafter (typically with a one-time connection charge of $25 or so for each line).

Savings: A family of four could potentially save up to $155 per month depending on their current service, or $1,860 per year.

16. Dump your bank.

When banks had free rein to hide fees in credit card charges, many provided free, basic services such as checking accounts.

Known as "interchange" fees, these tiny card charges made banks as much as $8.7 billion a year. (Of course, retailers hid the costs in these prices of the goods and services you bought.)

Federal reforms curbed the charges, but that meant rising bank fees. The first thing to go is likely to be free checking. You could pay up to $183 a year in banking fees if you're not already, bank experts say.

Instead, switch to a credit union. They offer truly free checking because the account holders, by definition, own the bank. You can find a local credit union at the National Credit Union Administration website (NCUA.gov).

Savings: If our sample couple had separate accounts that they close and merge into one at a credit union instead, that's $480 in savings per year.

17. Stop paying ATM fees.

Do you use ATMs? Consider this simple bit of math: If you take out $20 in a hurry at a convenience store and pay the fee — let's say the bank hits you for two dollars — you just gave it a fantastic deal — a nearly 10 percent return on cash. (I say "nearly," because the transaction costs the bank about 27¢.) Not to mention, banks are charging their account holders a fee for using foreign ATMs as well. That gravy train for the banks could be getting richer because some banks are considering five-dollar fees for non-customers.

Of course, the best solution is to plan ahead for cash needs and use only your bank's machines, where there is no fee. But if you don't use a credit union as suggested in the previous tip and instead opt for, say, an online investment brokerage that provides online banking services, you can find one that provides no-fee ATM use. Some providers of surcharge-free ATM cards include Fidelity.com, E*Trade.com, and Schwab.com.

Savings: If my family takes out money eight times a month, paying $2.50 a pop on average in fees, that's $240 a year.

18. Refinance revolving debt right now.

If you are holding credit card debt or a home equity loan at a high interest rate, now is the time to refinance. Credit card companies are still in the market for balance transfers that charge zero percent for up to two years and have no annual fees.

Savings: According to the Federal Reserve, a borrower with a credit card charging 19 percent must pay $202 a month on a $4,000 debt to be clear within two years. Taking out a zero percent card with a two-year window requires you to pay only $167 a month instead. The credit card savings amounts to $420.

19. Clean out your car's filter.

Gas and tolls are already costly enough. There's an easy way to save money every time you drive. Check your car manual for instructions on how to clear the air filter.

Savings: A clean air filter improves your gas mileage by up to seven percent, which translates into saving of about $100 for every 10,000 miles you drive.

20. Rethink your cable service.

If your cable, phone, and Internet services are bundled, call your provider to see if you're entitled to any promotional rates. Depending on where you live and whether there is competition, you may be able to negotiate either a lower rate or additional services. If you have a separate cable subscription, look into cutting back on the channels or cancelling cable altogether. After all, many programs are now available online.

Savings: In 2015, the average monthly cable bill is estimated to be $123. Over a year, cancelling cable would save you $1,476.

21. Use a rewards credit card if you pay your monthly balances in full.

I'm not a fan of credit cards because too many people don't have the discipline to pay off their balances. However, if you always make full payments each month, then you should use a credit card that features cash-back rewards. According to Bankrate.com, one in seven credit cards offered at least one percent back on all spending and nearly half of the reward cards offered a higher percentage in certain categories. Shop around for the card that offers the highest rewards for items you charge such as groceries, hotels, etc.

Savings: If you charge $5,000 each month on a card with a two percent cash-back offer, you would earn $100 that month, adding up to $1,200 over the course of a year. If you used a card that offered five percent cash-back on certain purchases per quarter, then you would earn even more.

22. Use the Entertainment Book or Groupon.com for travel, dining, goods, services, and more.

These discount books offer as much as 50 percent or more off ticket prices by city to zoos, museums, restaurants, movies, and many other activities. Likewise, you could find the same types of offers on Groupon.com. I use these discounts when I travel; by using the Entertainment coupons for just a few meals when you're away on vacation, you will have recouped the cost of the book. If you use Groupon, your up-front cost is the cost of the deal; in other words, the deal might be: pay $15 for a $30 dinner at XYZ Restaurant. For information, go to Entertainment.com and Groupon.com.

Savings: The percentage varies by coupon/deal; you can save as much as 50 percent or more off full price.

There Are Always Ways to Save Money

You may not believe me, but I started thinking of ways to make and save money when I was around five years old. I took a wagon and sold soda, and then when people asked if I could sell them beer, I took cans from my father's stash in the basement. My father thought I was crazy and tried to explain that I needed a license to sell liquor.

When I was around six, my father told me that he would pay me five dollars to cut the grass. When he came home a few hours later, I was sitting on the porch having lemonade while a friend of mine was mowing the lawn. My dad said, "I wanted to teach you about hard work and doing it yourself." Dad did teach me that, and I owe my work ethic and integrity to my parents' example. But at the time, I explained to my dad that I didn't mind working hard, but if given the choice, I'd rather not. I paid my pal $1.50 to mow the lawn and I kept $3.50 for myself. I learned that day that selling and negotiating pay more than working.

Appendix II: Most Frequently Asked Subscriber Questions

BY NOW YOU SHOULD have a very clear idea of how I pick stocks. I'm hoping that I've addressed any concerns about my strategy that may make you nervous. You shouldn't have any anxiety when you using *The Dividend Machine*. You should be relaxed, because you're confident that you've got the most experienced person guiding you through the markets.

Here are some of the questions (and my responses) that my readers have asked over the past few years:

Q: You always say, "Money you spend is money you're not investing." How do you decide whether spending on something is really important?

A: When I'm considering buying something, I always ask myself whether it will change my life. Am I buying this to satisfy an immediate need or some other purpose? For example, I recently bought my daughter a computer. At this stage of my life, I can buy whatever I want. But I still go through the exercise of asking whether I really need to buy this? Is it a want or a need?

If you find that you really don't need what you're considering buying, immediately put that money toward a long-term goal instead — whether it's paying for a private nursery school, your child's college tuition, or buying your dream home. In making a decision, think of how the purchase will affect you or your family. For example, you may get tired of a particular model car after a few years. But being able to pay for any college your child wants to attend would have a greater long-term impact.

You're either a spender or a saver. When you win a $500 jackpot, what do you do with the money? A friend of mine won $15,000 and immediately made plans to buy a new car, take his kids to Disney, and maybe save a thousand dollars. A person who's serious about finances would put $12,000 away and spend $3,000 to and take the kids to Disney. Someone serious about managing his money wouldn't spend the bulk of a sudden windfall.

Q: Can you explain how you evaluate how often you're going to use something in terms of justifying the expense?

A: My daughter will probably use her computer for another three to five years, so buying a more expensive, reliable model makes sense. But if she asked me to buy her a very expensive pair of boots, I might hesitate. After all, her feet could grow, the style could change, or she just might get tired of the boots. You need to factor in these kinds of considerations before you make an expensive purchase.

When you buy staples you invest in quality. If you're going to spend, make sure the purchase has meaning in your life and is something that will have a long-lasting impact.

People do things unconsciously. Millions of dollars are spent every year just because people aren't thinking. If you resist buying that $30,000 car, you could end up with $30 million in 20 years.

Q: **The advice in your newsletter seems to apply to not only investing, but other areas as well. Are you offering us life lessons?**

A: It's not only about the money. That's important, but there are also life lessons you have to learn and pass onto your children. It's about balance. You want your spiritual, physical, mental, emotional, and financial health all in unison. Life is a series of decisions based on self-control. Most people know right from wrong from the time they're five years old. People know when they shouldn't be spending money a lot of the time. How well can you control yourself?

Q: **When was the first time you made a major financial mistake? Were you able to turn it into a learning experience?**

A: I went back to school to get my teaching degree. I spent about $5,000, but it was hard to get a teaching job. I was trained in secondary education and business, and that was being phased out of the curriculum. I made a mistake. I spent money I shouldn't have spent. I should have taken the money I used to pay for school and invested it.

Thomas Edison made a thousand mistakes before he came up with the perfect prototype of the light bulb. Warren Buffett lost 20 percent of an investment he made in a gas station. Michael Jordan, the greatest basketball player of all time, says even he has missed ten thousand shots. In fact, he was cut from his high school basketball team as a sophomore.

I made mistakes early on. But I came back, started my business, and began planning for the future when I was in my 30s.

Q: What's do you think is the most important lesson that I can teach my children?

A: Learn to conquer your fears. Everybody gets afraid, but tenacity, faith in yourself, and guts get you through the hard times.

I never thought I was going to fail. I've fallen down many times, but I've always gotten back up — I always knew I was going to make millions of dollars. I knew I wasn't going to stop until I made it happen.

Q: Say I get a small sum of money together to begin investing based on your principles. How long will it take before I see results?

A: It might take a while. You don't start out as a heavyweight — you start as a lightweight.

If you can't get a couple thousand dollars together, you'll never be rich. But everyone can do it if they want to. Everyone can get rich. You just have to do a little something at a time and keep going. It's not about how hard you hit. It's about how hard you can get hit and keep moving forward. Life is about progressing, little by little. Start saving two bucks, then three bucks, and so on. Just keep going.

Q: I've always had a difficult time saving money. How do I change this life-long pattern?

A: Once you start saving money, it becomes an addiction. Every time you see what you've saved, you get addicted to saving more. Gradually, in all aspects of your life, you'll see ways to save and improve your finances. Again, I use the analogy of being on a diet or starting an exercise program. I improved my physical condition at age 50 when everyone said I couldn't do it. Of course I could. I started drinking more water and eating less junk. I learned to measure my steps and I began to walk more each day.

Q: You once gave criteria for a company explaining that, "If you can eat it, drink it, smoke it, or screw it, watch, wear, or bet on it, you have to get it. Altria was "Eat, drink, smoke." Why are you so focused on this approach?

A: If you want to avoid risk — the key tenet of *The Dividend Machine* — then you want to find a company that is recession-proof. That means people will always use that company's products regardless of world events. When times are bad, people still drink, smoke, watch TV, and wear clothing. On the other hand, you don't always drive a car. That's how I started my strategy; nobody liked those stocks and they were cheap. Now it's hard to buy them because that's where everyone wants to put their money. People buy Con Ed because they know the utility has been around for 130 years and isn't going out of business (we always need power).

I'm trying to make a machine that spits out enough money for you to retire. And, if the stock market crashes, you'll still be getting those dividends.

Q: How important is it to understand risk?

A: For me everything starts with assessing risk. The amateur looks at how much he can make. He moves toward things. The professional looks at what he can lose. If I think there's no way I can lose, I go. If you get a money-back guarantee, you're ready to buy something. You have no risk. There's no risk at all. Investors can choose a no-risk investment called

Treasury Bonds. The problem is they're paying .5 percent interest. I look at risk not as what I'm going to make, but where I'm not going to lose money. The upside may be capped, but the downside doesn't exist.

Q: How can the average person assess risk?

A: When you drive a car you have some degree of risk. You have to think about how fast you're driving compared to the chances of getting a ticket if you're speeding.

There's an inherent risk in investing just like in driving. You have to figure out the optimal speed. I don't pick the stock that yields the highest amount. I pick the one that won't lose. We have the aggressive stocks where you could lose money, but if you win, you make a lot of money. Only about five to ten percent of my portfolio is in aggressive holdings.

Q: Why do you look at things so much differently from most investors?

A: Most people can tell you what's happening. But when I tell people which stocks will go up, I tell them why. I do that by inverting — taking things back into reverse. It's not enough to memorize facts and figures. Each scenario is different. When you're investing, each company has a different group of parameters. You have to know what you're doing. I listen to different opinions about companies. Some billionaires invested heavily in JC Penney. But when a mother told me that she wasn't shopping there anymore because the store stopped offering coupons, my view of the stock completely changed. When you ask some billionaires why they invested in a particular stock, they often say, "Because I'm a billionaire." That's not a good enough answer for me.

Q: I recently began investing, and I was managing to keep my head above water by following market trends — doing what everyone else was doing. Why has this approach suddenly stopped working for me?

A: When you're an investor you have to tune out everything. Sometimes the best thing is to do nothing and sit down and analyze the company and do some research. Before you buy a stock you have to think it through. I always develop a strategy. Remember what your mom used to say: Just because your friends are doing it doesn't make it right.

Q: Is the ability to combine intuition and knowledge learned or innate?

A: Honestly, I think you can learn how to do this. You can learn how to do this provided you've had the life experiences. It was easier for me because I've been gambling since I was a little boy. Buffett did too.

Q: How can I invest if I'm carrying debt?

A: Not all debt is something to get nervous about. It's just another thing you need to keep track of. If you have debt, obviously you want to pay off the debt with the highest interest rate. Borrowing is all about how cheap the money is. If you're borrowing money at 20 percent, you'd better restructure it. You should worry about the debt you're carrying with interest rates of 18 percent or higher.

Q: Can you get started investing later in life?

A: I was 30 when I started my dividend strategy. My goal was to be able to stop working in seven years. It took 13 years, but it worked. I do think it's better to start investing when you're younger. Starting before you have children is particularly smart. Once you have children, you have more expenses.

Speaking of children, I encourage parents to borrow as much as possible, depending on the interest rate, to pay for college tuition. If you can borrow at a rate under three or four percent, do so, provided you can invest the money you would have otherwise spent and earn 12 percent.

Unless you or your child is attending law or medical school, going into debt in order to attend school isn't smart. Alternatives include working first to save money to pay for school or attending a community college. Maybe get a grant. My friend's daughter got a job at the Marriott to pay her way through college and it took her six years to finish school. But she finished and did well. Her father took the money that would have gone to tuition and invested it in a dividend machine for her. Now she's sitting on a six-figure portfolio that is still growing very nicely.

Q: What is the difference between investing and speculating?

A: Here's the key difference between the investor and the speculator: The speculator only cares about the price of a stock. Speculators will buy at a specific price and sell it at another price. The investor doesn't pay attention to the stock price. The real investor hopes it goes down so he can buy it cheaper with all the money he's saving. The investor cares about what the company is doing. Value will be found out later. In the short term, the market is a voting machine — a barometer of what people think. In the long term, it's a weighing machine.

Speculation is what the average person does when he or she invests. You say that you want your $10,000 investment to become $200,000 overnight. However, that's not how the market works. It's not realistic and isn't going to happen. If that's your approach, then you might as well go to a casino and have a good time . . . because you probably won't earn $200,000 there either.

Q: **What should kids and teens know about investing?**

A: Investing is the number one ticket to making a new life for yourself or a good life for your kid. And, you can teach your kids about investing. Investing can be really fun. Make it into a game for them. The trick is to get them into predicting something. Let them predict the weather, or try betting on the Oscars — so they learn not only how to get it right, but also how to make mistakes. Pick a company they like, such as Abercrombie & Fitch or Apple if your kids use iPhones. Make investing something that they understand because it's connected to their world. If they can grasp that investing is about picking brands or entities that interest you for compelling reasons, and that you have to make predictions about their value based on a bunch of variables, you've taught them investing.

For example, make the lesson kid-friendly by saying that Oreo stock would do well if the cookie part is nice and crispy but badly if it's soggy. If you give the kid a soggy Oreo, then ask if he or she would invest in Oreos. Chances are your kid is going to understand the concept and you've just conveyed a very important lesson to them, not just about investing, but about so many other things in life that require analysis of a situation.

Remember that brokerages require investors to be at least 18 years old to conduct transactions, so while your kids can choose stocks, you will have to buy them if they're not yet 18 years old.

Q: How long should you hold onto stocks to maximize profits?

A: I give each investment three to five years. The price itself doesn't determine whether I'll sell the stock before then, but if the reasons I bought the stock change, then I may decide to sell. For example, if I really admire a CEO's strategy and the CEO gets hit by a car, then I would probably sell the stock.

Appendix III:
Subscriber Testimonials

Bill Garcia:

I recommended *The Dividend Machine* newsletter to everybody. Everyone thinks Bill Spetrino is my neighbor — that's how close we are. All of my friends feel like they know Bill because I talk about him all of the time.

Some people just don't believe it when I tell them that you're not sending him any money — you are investing it on your own. Bill gives you honest information, he's down to earth, and he speaks your language.

The $100 investment is the best I've ever made. He has actually stimulated my mind to think more in terms of financial investment and stocks more so than ever before. So, not only am I getting a great return on my investments, but I'm getting an education along the way and it's very consistent with my values. He keeps it simple. He is not complicated. He makes it seem as if you are going shopping at the grocery store or clothing store.

The Dividend Machine is paying for my vacations, for the gifts that I give to people. I'm going to Greece in June with my wife. We're taking a trip to Alaska at the beginning of June. I'm going to Cabo in April with my brother. So, we're doing a lot of neat things that I never thought I was going to be able to do.

I didn't grow up wealthy at all. I grew up in the inner city in Los Angeles. My mother was a seamstress and we all had to work together at the end of the day sewing and making clothing, so *The Dividend Machine* is just opening up my eyes. I'm telling my entire family that Bill's newsletter can really change your life financially, and if you're not doing *The Dividend Machine*, you're making one of the biggest mistakes of your life, and I honestly believe that.

I've done well financially over the years because of what I've done. I was Vice President of the Xerox Corporation, but not because of my investments, you know. Now, I feel like I can do well through investments with my retirement. I feel at this point, with Bill Spetrino, I'm going to be able to make more money than I ever was able to make. I'm a church going guy, so I go to church every Sunday and I'm a full tithe-payer, and my goal is to be able to tithe what I was tithing when I was working for Xerox Corporation, and I know with Bill Spetrino I'll be able to do that.

I said earlier that there are a couple of individuals who are very important in my life: my wife, of course, my pastor, my doctor, and then there is Bill Spetrino, and it has even gotten to the point where I trust Bill more than I trust my doctor. And there's no question about that, because Bill has given me results, but my doctor has let me down a few times.

Jay Coffsky:

How much money does a person need to start *The Dividend Machine*? Well, of course, that varies, but I've started my eight grandchildren with about $10,000 a piece with dividend-machine stocks, and what I've done is I've kind of divided that into three or four stocks and every time I have a birthday or a celebration I'll buy them one or two shares of each of those stocks as their present. I think they are going to learn that they can do their own dividend machine before they are 20 years old.

In the last 2.5 years, my portfolio has returned actually close to $1,000,000 and I was about to . . . at some point I hope to write Bill a letter or an e-mail to let him know I don't really need the extra $1,000,000. I mean I could always use it. My children will enjoy it, but it is a feeling of being on air so to speak. I can do anything that I want. I don't have to answer to anybody. I'm still looking for an agenda, but Bill has no agenda — that's what is so beautiful about *The Dividend Machine.*

All of my accounts are with the same broker and I look at activity and some days there is no activity, but other days there is a lot. One day, recently, I had $10,000 come in; it was like getting a check or going on a cruise and putting some down on a roulette wheel and winning. I mean, I didn't do anything to get this money and all of a sudden $10,000 popped in there one day. It makes you feel real good and, you know, the rest of the day could go bad, but you won't forget how that day started off pretty good. And so every day I check it, and five, six, or more times a month, money shows up from one of these dividends, and I say, "Wow, man — this is like owning property!"

You know I found Bill Spetrino and *The Dividend Machine* strictly by accident. It wasn't unusual to kind of surf the internet for dividend stocks and just put dividends into the web browser, and one day it came up, and I don't really know how long *The Dividend Machine* had been around, but I had never heard of it before. So I clicked on the site and it looked pretty good and it was pretty cheap compared to other subscriptions. I think it was about $99 and most of the others were $200, $300, $400 and I said, you know, I'll try it. I tried it thinking it was going to be like most of the others that would attempt to upsell you or had some agenda. Like I said, I couldn't find another agenda. Even Morningstar, one of the great investment letters, keeps calling all of the time trying to sell you other services. I never got that from *The Dividend Machine.*

Our pension manager at the time was a very educated person who would give us these long charts, which I really never understood. With *The Dividend Machine*, the newsletter has good information that I can understand. Almost anybody who knows anything about money management at all can understand it and it has been consistent and the results have been excellent.

Pat Sugrue:

I discovered *The Dividend Machine* and started researching Bill Spetrino and his theories and ideas on investing. It became clear to me that his philosophy of reinvesting dividends and building this machine to generate cash over a period of time was a winning one. It was so simple, but yet powerful to see that power of reinvested dividends.

I've invested in several different stocks recommended in the newsletters, but a couple of specific ones have earned more than a 100 percent return. And my portfolio has gone up by more than 44 percent (and my wife's has gone up by 47 percent) and I'm just overwhelmed by the fact that something that seems so simple has been able to be that successful.

The newsletter gave me the confidence to buy stocks, so my advisor actually called me and asked them why I was suddenly buying individual stocks. I told them about *The Dividend Machine* and mentioned Bill Spetrino's name, and his thought process on reinvesting dividends and buying conservative stocks that have a long track record of dividend payments as well as some of the almost instant success that I'd had with a couple of my selections. I said that I slept better knowing that I was invested in these and following this plan than I had been just sitting in cash and they were quite taken aback by the fact that I was deciding to do this on my own versus using a managed portfolio plan that he offered me for a fee.

The newsletter is something that I look forward to receiving every month. It's one of the first things I open and it's a very easy read. Bill interjects a lot of humor and real life situations that I enjoy, as he makes analogies and comparisons between investing and sports, his life growing up, and some of the different challenges he had understanding and making market decisions. The newsletter, podcast, and weekly market updates are other things that, in my opinion, just give me more confidence that what he is doing is helping me to secure my future.

I personally didn't feel I was smart enough to make these decisions on my own either, but *The Dividend Machine* gave me the security and confidence to follow a person whose sound advice would make me comfortable enough to even put my parent's money in to invest with. His analysis and his track record shows me that this person really cares about what he does and cares about peoples' financial future, and yet he's not asking anyone to take a lot of risk.

He doesn't overload you with dozens and dozens of stocks; Bill's strategy has been very consistent, with a certain number of stocks in his conservative portfolio. He offers you a few selections in an aggressive portfolio as well as a few suggestions that you might want to consider in this international portfolio, but Bill's main drive is putting 90 percent of your money in a conservative portfolio.

Paul Jonson:

I don't know if I can express in words what Bill Spetrino has brought to my life in regards to the investment area. Using his methodology and his guidance really saved me from the continued investment follies that I would have followed over the years. He changed my life for the positive and I would be in investment purgatory if not for him. I want to thank him for setting me on the right course — the prudent investment course of investing in fundamentally strong companies that pay dividends and increase those dividends over time so not only do I get the growth of the stock market, but I get the increase in dividends so while I'm sleeping I'm earning money.

It is very enjoyable to read and it is very user friendly because Bill speaks in a language and explains things that everybody can understand.

People are stuck. They don't know what to do, and I call it paralyses by analysis; take a step, buy the stock, get your machine rolling and the next thing you know you'll be riding down easy street and you will be so happy that you did.

With *The Dividend Machine* I feel like John Rockefeller. One of my favorite times is when the dividends roll in on a quarterly basis. I just love looking at the upward growth of my dividend machine. My holdings are growing incrementally with each reinvested dividend and I think it is great that I get paid to own shares in a company.

I think the biggest improvement in my life since I've developed my dividend machine is peace of mind because I don't have to worry about the latest investment fad, and I don't have to get up and look at the stock market every day. I know that I have invested in strong fundamental companies that pay a dividend that increases over time and that my whole machine is going to increase in value quarter after quarter after quarter. I have to continue to look at it and follow Bill's advice and his guidance and see if it still meets within my own investment expectation because we all know that bulls and bears make money, and pigs get lead to slaughter.

One stock was up 67 percent and another stock was up 31 percent and another stock was up 33 percent and another stock was up 25 percent and another stock is up 15 percent and one I have is it is up only nine percent, but I have it for the yield, which is over five percent right now. So, I have been very happy with my dividend portfolio!

Mark Tretter:

I am a 59-year-old retiree who has worked 60 hours a week since age 18, either at two or more jobs or as owner/manager of several restaurants. I left college without graduating to own and run a restaurant. After 10 years of running restaurants, I'm tired of the constant turmoil. I changed directions and worked as a food service manager at a local retirement village and hospital until debilitating back problems forced me to take early retirement.

After rolling my 401(k) and 403(b) accounts into an IRA and the inheritance from my father into a taxable account at a local brokerage, I followed my broker's advice and put the monies into mutual funds and individual dividend blue-chip stocks. I watched the mutual funds grow slowly compared to the stocks, at much higher fees, and realized that I could accumulate faster with stocks. I started picking stocks based on what their dividend paid with little focus on their fundamentals.

This was just before the recession; things were going great and I had a nice dividend income from picking the high-yield dividend suggested by all the so called "experts'" online publications.

Then the recession hit; the stocks tanked, and worse yet, they decreased or totally cut their dividends! My income dropped by half and my holdings depreciated as well. About this time I found Bill Spetrino's *Dividend Machine*, a select list of dividend large-cap stocks that weathered the recession much better than my previous holdings had done. Their two to five percent dividends were paltry against the 10 to 20 percent stocks that I had before, but these stocks not only held their value in bad times, they also consistently raised their dividends every year!

Bill's not only recommended the stocks to buy but said what price to buy them at and what proportion of your portfolio to hold. He also gave notice as to when to sell. Prior to following his newsletter, more often than not I had capital losses at year-end from chasing high-yield stocks. Now, my portfolio has gained 15-20 percent for the last three years! I especially like the weekly newsletter he publishes in addition to the monthly, and the actionable recommendations he gives on all his newsletters. He has conservative, aggressive, and international portfolios. I'm mostly invested in his conservative and it has consistently out-performed any of my holdings prior to getting his publications. I have also done well in the aggressive and international picks. The key to success that he stresses is to buy quality stocks at the right price, which he provides. I can honestly say my holdings have dramatically increased and that I sleep much better at night using Bill's picks than any other publication!

W. D. Meadows:

I started my subscription in 2010 and purchased Altria (MO) at $16. My wife and I have investments at several major brokerage firms and had many stocks in accordance with their recommendations. They asked me to consider selling the MO on several occasions, but I disagreed and held it. On a few occasions I discussed individual recommendations from *The Dividend Machine* with these major Wall Street firms and they talked me out of them — what a mistake that was!!!!

After over $100,000 in accumulated losses at one firm, I fired them and transferred those assets to Fidelity where I made further investments in the stocks recommended by Mr. Spetrino. In 2013 my wife and I were up over 30 percent — trouncing the hedge funds who charge us a fortune in fees! That return is in line with the "market" for 2013, but that's irrelevant. If you look at the indices over recent years they have had some gut-wrenching volatility that I just can't stand anymore — not after the dot-com bubble in 2000, the housing crash of 2006, and the recession of 2009. Furthermore, I can't build a significant dividend income stream with a market-tracking index fund — replacing my current income for retirement — which of course is the central tenet of *The Dividend Machine* philosophy!

We love Bill's solid, deliberate, and articulate way of teaching us about investing, and his thought process as he makes individual recommendations. We love the deep-value selection process modeled after the techniques of famous investors such as Benjamin Graham and Warren Buffett. Bill's clarity and big-picture thinking cuts through the confusion put out by the TV pundits; he speaks in plain English and NOT Wall Street gibberish, not to impress us, but to teach and explain his reasoning behind each investment selection — refreshing compared to the confusion put out by Wall Street analysts who want to keep us confused so we need them and keep paying their ridiculous fees!

What a valuable newsletter and a ridiculous bargain for the price! By the way, I pay at least two grand for a chairman's club subscription to *Real Money* and *IBD*. I am scaling those back drastically because I get more out of Bill's newsletter, the weekly updates, and weekly podcasts, following both his stock picks and, more importantly, his lessons in patience.

I could go on and on but give it a try and look at his numbers — they are there for ANYONE to see.

Robert Hockensmith, CPA:
My investment outlook has vastly improved since 2010, when I started subscribing to Bill's newsletter. I've actually made over $170,000 in that short period of time just by buying the investments that Bill has suggested. I look at it now as though I've gotten a reprieve — I have a second chance to actually retire at an earlier age, if I so choose, from the kind of investing portfolio that Bill has suggested.

The Dividend Machine has made me more confident. Prior to subscribing, I would pick the investments that I thought had good basics and I'd do well sometimes and do terrible sometimes, but I now see far more consistency. I have not invested in one single

stock that has lost money using *The Dividend Machine*. Now I
have a better idea of how to pick my investments, and I also recognize that this is going to take time. I can think about whether I
want to sell and keep that profit, or split off but keep the stocks.

The Dividend Machine is not just a newsletter; it's a group of
people that actually care about your success. With other newsletters, 80 percent of the revenues come from the actual commissions off the newsletters and 20 percent from actual investments
by the writer, while 97 percent of the income that comes from Mr.
Spetrino comes from him investing; not from his commissions off
the investors.

Bill puts the dividend investing program into very simple
terms. I teach at the university level, but I've taught at the high
school level and in the military as well. He is good about explaining it in very simple terms so that anybody will understand.

Kelly Erickson:

I followed your advice to buy Altria when it was $19. It was my
first stock purchase ever. I loaded the boat! You recommended it
to be 20 percent of my portfolio. I followed that recommendation
exactly. Of course now it is worth 20 percent because of reinvested dividends and subsequent purchases. I have had over 100 percent return on my initial investment with reinvested dividends.

Of course, this is only one company. When I started with *The
Dividend Machine* three years ago, I bought every conservative
stock in the model portfolio with appropriate weighed percentages. Every single conservative selection has been a winner! If
you were a hitter in baseball .250 is good, .300 is great, .400 (Ted
Williams) is out of this world . . . What would we say about you
batting 1.000? As one who has coached baseball for years (hitting
primarily), I know the hard work and discipline it takes to be a
great hitter.

Well, the beauty of *The Dividend Machine* is, as Bill has
said in his newsletters, that it's built like a tank, so whether the

economy is great or bad, it's going to weather the storm. Investing in solid companies that have the financial wherewithal to navigate through good times and the bad times allows me to sleep well at night knowing my portfolio is doing exactly what it's meant to. I look at it daily, but I don't have to. I have peace and comfort knowing that it's doing what it's designed to do.

And that is the cool thing — I'm looking at my portfolio and they're all winners. The only losers I've had are when I've taken the advice of other people. Bill works very hard to ensure that his subscribers don't lose money and that's the key. He wants to help us grow our wealth, but he also doesn't want to lose us money.

I don't have the time to spend hours to dissect companies so I'm glad I can pay somebody a small fee — an annual small fee — to do the heavy lifting for me. That is awesome!

Greg Hanner:

Bill has an in-your-face writing style. I love it because I don't have a lot of time. I want to know: What do I need to know this week? This month? And he comes right at you with the facts, explaining the situations in terms of current events for the individual plays and adjusts his buy prices. You can't just go and get one copy of the newsletter and think you have the playbook. Getting those updates from Bill on an ongoing basis is critical and I love it.

What I would say to somebody who thinks he or she is too old to get started in *The Dividend Machine* is don't walk in my footsteps, because if I could do it all over again I would have started 10 or 15 years ago. The power is having the "key to the mint," so to speak. It's in starting at some point — start small with whatever you can and just let it build. It's not something you have to worry about. The sooner you start the better your results are going to be when you do need the money. We are all going to get old and as you get older, it will be too late to start trying to create dividend yield and cash flow for retirement. A younger person has got a heck of an advantage because he or she has time on their side.

The beauty of *The Dividend Machine* newsletter is that you don't have to be a rocket scientist. Bill does the hard work. Bill spends countless hours — hundreds and hundreds of hours — studying the particular play. He's already made the mistakes, so learning from a master like Bill is empowering.

The one thing that I want people to know about the newsletter is that it is not filled with difficult concepts. It's probably one of the easiest and most affordable tools you can use rather than hearing somebody else's opinion (a friend, a relative) who has a different risk tolerance, a different net worth, maybe a different time-horizon than yours. He's your safety pilot. He's not going to let you crash and burn. He's not going to have you go into something that's a high-beta play that has no earnings to back up the play.

The Dividend Machine really can help boost the confidence of a trader or investor because of the matter-of-fact, Cliff's-Notes style of Bill's writing. Bill gets right to the point. You don't have to do all of the plays. I choose to do quite a few of them, but if you just get a few good ideas out of it, I can't see how you won't be successful using *The Dividend Machine*.

Art Riccio:

I have been investing in the stock market for over 40 years and I have bought numerous investment newsletters. *The Dividend Machine* is the best in the business for serious long-term investors. There's no stock of the month gimmicks; no high-risk speculative junk; no in and out trading — just plain, old, sound investing advice and worthwhile investment recommendations.

Following Spetrino's advice will result in long-term financial security with an income stream that will let you finally have your money working for you. He does what you thought your stock broker or other letter-writers were going to do for you but didn't. All your broker wanted was to make a sales commission off of you. All the other letter-writers wanted was to suck you in with a cheap letter and then sell you a higher-priced letter or rope you into their commission-based, money management company. All you need is a discount broker to dollar-cost average into Spetrino's recommendations and you will become financially secure over time.

I've been around the financial block many times and know what works and what doesn't. I know the game and the BS that is spewed by the financial community. I wish I had found this guy and his letter 40 years ago. It would have saved me a lot of time and money and would have made me a ton more money earlier in my stock investing career. I had to learn what Spetrino preaches on my own. He will help you earn a very high and safe annual rate of return, especially once the compounding and growth of the dividend stream kicks in.

If you're a trader, gambler, speculator, or just the typical retail investor who thinks he is smarter than the Wall Street pros who have been eating your lunch all of these years, then go somewhere else as Spetrino's advice will bore the hell out of you. If you want to lose your money and have excitement, better yet, go to a casino. But if you want to get rich slowly but surely and have a great retirement, I suggest you go with Spetrino. By the way, I don't get squat for writing this. I took the time to write this because it is nice after all these years to finally find someone who cares about helping the little guy in the market.

Gary McCartney:

My investment story would begin with how one of my best friends asked me to invest in a business opportunity. I flew from Florida to Washington for a meeting — all expenses paid. There was a big office and other investors had made good money. It all sounded good and of course, my friend was very successful, driving exotic sports cars and more. I put in a large chunk of money, but after two years of promises, it turned out it was a Ponzi scheme.

My friend said how he had no idea. Of course, he wanted to make it up to me and told me about another guaranteed investment. My friend is very convincing and he was a very good friend, so again I invested, and again, it was a Ponzi scheme. My "friend" turned out to be no friend at all; he was a big scammer and is now serving time.

I needed to find something I could do to make money. I don't care for financial advisors since they are just interested in making money off you. I joined some financial newsletters and even a short-term, swing-trading chatroom. Again, everything always sounds so good. But again I lost my money. The people who write the newsletters are a bunch of clowns, not even investing in what they are telling you to buy.

Then I found Bill Spetrino's *Dividend Machine*. The reviews I read were solid and I liked the investing approach he has. Bill puts his money where his mouth is. I joined in December 2011 and I have earned more than I could have imagined. I can see how this WILL make up for all the losses I had. I have already averaged over 20 percent annual returns. I am very excited knowing I am part of a DIVIDEND MACHINE that will continue to GROW and create an income for my family.

This is one of those moments in your life when you say, "IF ONLY I HAD KNOWN SOONER!!"

Thank you Bill, you have made a difference in my family's and my life!

Forever Grateful.

ABOUT THE AUTHOR

BILL SPETRINO IS THE editor of Newsmax' advisory service, *The Dividend Machine*. Bill's goal is to show the average investor how they can generate a substantial monthly income by investing in high-quality dividend-paying companies.

A native of Cleveland, Ohio, Spetrino graduated from John Carroll University with a degree in accounting. Bill's wife is a CPA, and he assisted her in her private accounting and tax planning practice.

It was during this time that Spetrino began studying the investing philosophies of some of the world's greatest investors, including Warren Buffett and Sir John Templeton. By learning, and then implementing, the lessons of these great investors, he has been able to build a truly impressive investment portfolio of his own.

Spetrino brings you all of his knowledge and experience identifying the strongest dividend-paying companies in the financial world. He shares this information to help members build their own "dividend machine" and enjoy the investing success he has experienced over the past 20 years.

INDEX